The Crowning Venture

Inspiration from Women Who Have Memorized the Quran

Dr. Saadia Mian lives in Michigan where she works full-time as an endocrinologist. After completing an undergraduate degree in psychology at the University of Michigan, she went to medical school at Michigan State University.

During that same time she traveled to Syria to study Arabic, Quran, and sacred knowledge. She received her *ijāza* in the Ḥafṣ recitation of Quran from Shaykh Abu Hassan Al-Kurdi (May Allah be pleased with him) and also from Shaykh Krayyim Rajih. She completed the memorization of the Quran and is currently working on obtaining an *ijāza ʿal-ghaib* (*ijāza* in memorization). She helped to launch the Ribaat Quran program and teaches *tajwīd* for Ribaat.

She is a member of the founding board of Rabata and continues to serve while doing all the other things she loves like helping people with their health, traveling, writing, spending time with her sisters, nieces, and nephews, and drinking chai with her parents.

THE CROWNING VENTURE

Inspiration from Women Who Have Memorized the Quran

Ḥāfiẓa Saadia Mian, MD

Daybreak Press

The Crowning Venture by Saadia Mian
First printed in 2018

Published by:
Daybreak Press
Minneapolis, Minnesota, USA
Rabata.org/Daybreak-Press

Library of Congress Control Number: 2018943576
ISBN: 978-0-9992990-3-6

Cover design by Reyhana Ismail (reyoflightdesign.com)
Cover illustration by Niky Motekallem (nikymotekallem.com)
Book design and typesetting by scholarlytype.com
Set in Cormorant Garamond 11/13

Printed in the United States of America

Dedicated to my parents

Naseem Akhtar Mian and Muhammad Rafiq Mian

for their love and endless support, even when
I took the 'road less traveled'

Special Thanks to

Tamara Gray
for her guidance in this endeavor and the one called 'life'

Najiyah Maxfield-Helwani
for being the best editor I could ask for and for encouraging me to continue every time I freaked out about sharing my personal journey

Rydanah Dahman
for her help in finding books with key information about the memorization of Quran

Marah Dahman
for helping me find sources of hadith

Raghad al-Sayyid
for helping with translating original texts from Arabic

Sana Mohiuddin
for helping find sources of hadith

Eamaan Rabbat
for helping with transliteration

Nosaiba Hakim
for helping with translating original texts in Arabic

Munazza (Baj), Fadiyah, Anam,
Maryam, Yusuf, Iman, Taha, Nusaybah, Aisha, Hafsah,
Muhammad, Hiba and Fatima
for their love and support and for keeping me on my toes!

Contents

بسم الله الرحمن الرحيم

وَلَقَدْ يَسَّرْنَا ٱلْقُرْءَانَ لِلذِّكْرِ فَهَلْ مِن مُّدَّكِرٍ

Introduction

And We have certainly made the Quran easy for remembrance,
so is there any who will remember?

Quran: 54:17

It leaves me speechless when I reflect on the *ḥāfiẓāt*—women who have memorized the Quran. They are, without doubt, women of great courage, light, and blessing.

Who is memorizing the Quran? What different methodologies do women employ, and what are some tips to aid in this endeavor? I know in my own journey with the Quran that I have had my personal shortcuts and long, drawn-out, heart-wrenching struggles. It is an experience like no other. Yet I have found that few women venture forth on this memorization path, and I've often wondered why. What are the hurdles they face, and who creates them?

The pages of this book are filled with the stories of women who did undertake the journey of memorizing Quran. These real-life stories are both a map for other Muslim women who wish to travel this adventurous route and a record and witness to the many Muslim women who are the *ḥāfiẓāt* of this *umma*.

For many of the women mentioned in these pages, memorizing the entire Quran was not part of their life plan or even on their radar. Each one of them had a somewhat different path to the Quran, but many echoed similar sentiments about their journey. They spoke of falling in "love" with the Quran, of forming an attachment like one might with a close friend, and of no longer being able to imagine life without it.

In this book, I share with you their stories. I also explore questions around why more women do not memorize the Quran. I have heard women and girls being told they should not memorize the Quran for a myriad of reasons such as, "Women get too busy with housework and won't have time to review," and "Women don't lead *tarāwīḥ*, so why would they need to memorize the Quran?" And of course there is the one that discourages the strongest of heart, "It's worse to memorize and then forget it than to never memorize it at all." All of these disheartening notions were thrown aside by the women I interviewed. They found the path of least resistance and became walking Qurans.

While I was memorizing Quran in Syria, I often heard the following hadith. It gave me an image to hold in my mind and hope to hold in my heart. Muʿādh b. Anas ﵁ stated that the Messenger of God ﷺ said, "Whoever recites the Quran and acts according to what it contains, God will adorn his parents with a crown on the Day of Judgement, its radiance more beautiful than the radiance of the sun in the abode of this world. So what do you presume [the reward will be] for the one who acts according to it?"[1]

عن معاذ بن أنس رضي الله عنه أن رسول الله صلى الله عليه وسلم قال: مَنْ قَرَأَ الْقُرْآنَ وَعَمِلَ بِمَا فِيهِ أُلْبِسَ وَالِدَاهُ تَاجًا يَوْمَ الْقِيَامَةِ ضَوْءُهُ أَحْسَنُ مِنْ ضَوْءِ الشَّمْسِ فِي بُيُوتِ الدُّنْيَا لَوْ كَانَتْ فِيكُمْ فَمَا ظَنُّكُمْ بِالَّذِي عَمِلَ بِهَذَا

That was not the last I heard about crowns though. Any time someone received their *ijāza* in *tajwīd* or in memorization, my teachers threw elaborate parties for them. The recipients would wear beautiful, flowing white gowns and faux-diamond and pearl-embedded crowns on top of their heads. These women, with the glow of the Quran on their faces, would then give speeches sharing their stories with the Quran, after which everyone rejoiced with songs and good food. The crown of the Day of Judgement became a real crown we could all see. The title of this book reflects this image: The Crowning Venture. I hope and pray it will be a venture that more women will undertake, so that we can stand together, crowned and crowning our parents, on the Day we meet our Lord.

I interviewed more than twenty women for this book. Each one was gracious and open with me about her experience. Their names have been changed, as well as geographic and personal details, to protect their privacy. I have also changed the names and personal details of my teachers (other than Anse Tamara who is a public figure) in order to respect their privacy. While not every story made it into the book as a full story, each is reflected in later chapters that address methodologies and tips around memorizing. I am grateful to each one of them and encouraged by their stories. I hope and pray that this book will be the beginning of your story—the story of every Muslim woman and how she walked on her own crowning venture.

Venture: a risky or daring journey

Chapter One
My Venture

The Prophet ﷺ said,

"I saw the pillar of the Book (the Quran), taken from below my head; so I followed it with my eyes until it reached Syria..."

عَنْ أَبِي الدَّرْدَاءِ، قَالَ: قَالَ رَسُولُ اللهِ صَلَّى اللهُ عَلَيْهِ وَسَلَّمَ: بَيْنَا أَنَا نَائِمٌ إِذْ رَأَيْتُ عَمُودَ الْكِتَابِ احْتُمِلَ مِنْ تَحْتِ رَأْسِي ، فَظَنَنْتُ أَنَّهُ مَذْهُوبٌ بِهِ ، فَأَتْبَعْتُهُ بَصَرِي ، فَعُمِدَ بِهِ إِلَى الشَّامِ...

Prophet Muhammad ﷺ[2]

We know that Allah's ﷻ plan for us is greater than anything we can imagine for ourselves. Never does this become more apparent to me than when I reflect on my journey with the Quran. Growing up in a small town in Michigan with very few Muslim families and no Islamic center, I lived the kind of life any daughter of Pakistani immigrants would live. I went to school (was expected to do well, of course), prayed and fasted Ramadan, and was taught to love and revere the Prophet ﷺ.

The closest Islamic center was an hour's drive away, and we attended Sunday school there for a few years, until that fell by the wayside. Pakistani culture insists that children read through the entire Quran at least once. So, as a dutiful daughter, I read it and had my 'Ameen' party. I was eight years old. We had cake and gifts, and I was proud to have accomplished the goal that had been set for me. After that I did not pick up the Quran to read it much at all. As time passed and I entered high school, I immersed myself in my studies and focused on excelling in tennis and soccer. I had a habit of throwing myself fully into anything I did, and I was soon the number one doubles player on the tennis team and made the varsity soccer team in my sophomore year. Later, I would use this personality quirk on my journey with the Quran, but for now, reading the Quran regularly—let alone memorizing it—was the farthest thing from my mind. I had only met one woman in all those years who had memorized the entire Quran, and she was someone to whom, although I respected her greatly, I could not relate.

The Venture Begins

My journey on a serious path to Allah ﷻ began at the same time that my relationship with the Quran started. It was the same summer I met my teachers and decided that this traditional method of learning was the path I wanted to take to Allah ﷻ. For me, the two experiences are one and the same. They were and are intertwined and affected each other.

My journey to the Quran began outside of my usual careful planning. I did not fit the picture I had in my mind of what a *ḥāfiẓa* looked like. In my mind, a *ḥāfiẓa* would be a highly respected religious figure who had unending religious knowledge, was dressed in traditional clothing like a *jilbāb,* and would have to be a perfect Muslim. I did not feel like a perfect Muslim and, therefore, I did not imagine myself as a *ḥāfiẓa*. Sometimes, the only way I can describe it is that the Quran drew me close to it itself. Pulled me in. Reading Quran was not like reading any other book. I felt like it was a real conversation. And it had a magnetism that increased as I read. The more I read, the more I wanted to read.

It all started with a desire to learn Arabic toward the end of my undergraduate years, before starting medical school. For me, college was a time to explore what my religion meant to me and how I wanted to live as a Muslim. As the years passed, I realized I wanted to do more than just increase my practice; I wanted to know why I was doing what I was doing. I needed to *know.* After having spent those years focused on getting into medical school, I had reached a point of yearning for something I felt was missing from my life. I was looking for something deeper. In most of the lectures I heard on campus, a common theme was the importance of learning Arabic to be able to understand the Quran without translation. I took those words to heart and prayed for a door to open for me to learn fluent Arabic. That door came in the guise of the eight months I had in between graduating college and starting medical school. I started a correspondence course in Arabic and then entertained the idea of traveling to an Arabic-speaking country to facilitate my learning.

Opportunity Shows Itself

During this time, a young woman I knew from college returned from a trip to Damascus, Syria, where she had learned Arabic and *tajwīd* and gotten her *ijāza*. *Tajwīd* is the science of the pronunciation of the Quran, and the *ijāza* system is traditional Islamic learning where, after thorough study and testing, the student becomes a teacher. I was intrigued by her *ijāza* and interested in *tajwīd*. I joined a learning circle with her and her lessons began building upon the basic *tajwīd* I had learned when I was younger.

There was an interesting and positive change in my friend. At the time I struggled to put it into words, but looking back, she had returned from Syria with a new sense of sincerity and a more 'down to earth' aura surrounded her. Every so often she spoke of her teachers in Syria, and I was curious to hear more about these women who were scholars. As I deliberated and wondered about traveling myself, her experiences gave me courage and conviction that I too, could travel abroad for Arabic and Quran.

When it came time to decide which country to go to, I decided on Syria so I could fulfill my dream of being able to learn from female scholars. This was in 1998, and the idea of women teachers was novel and almost unheard of. I hoped to bring my new-found knowledge and experience back to my own community of sisters.

Damascus

After much deliberation and one failed attempt, I found myself headed for Damascus. I was a bit nervous, not knowing what to expect, but I was blessed to board the plane with two acquaintances who were on similar knowledge-seeking paths. After arriving at the Damascus airport, some friends of one of my travel partners picked us up and deposited us in the middle of the night at an apartment in Mezze, a suburb of Damascus.

The city was noisy and awake. Tall buildings standing at attention and micro-buses crowded with people. I was used to small-town Michigan, with its quiet streets and organized crosswalks. I started to wonder what I had gotten myself into.

As I was jetlagged, I didn't sleep that night. I stepped out on the balcony that overlooked the neighboring mosque, al-Akram, and listened to the sounds of the city. Nervous as I was, the green lights shining from the many minarets gave me a feeling that I was embarking on something special.

The *Ijāza*

My initial goal had been Arabic. Though I had been impressed by my friend's accomplishments with the Quran, I had not imagined myself following in those footsteps. I didn't have enough time, it wasn't on my "radar," and I really didn't think I was capable. My focus changed one day when Anse Tamara Gray sat with all the newcomers and asked us to recite from anywhere in the Quran. After hearing my recitation, she asked if I would be interested in getting my *ijāza* in *tajwīd*. I jumped at the chance, immediately rewiring my goals and aspirations for those few months, and reminded myself that my friend back home, who was Indian-American, had been able to do it. My mind went on high speed as I began to think about all the details. Who would my teacher be? How much would it cost? What would be the first step, etc.

After I was assigned a teacher, I had the uncomfortable task of talking about money. I asked Anse Tamara how much the fee would be for my teacher, and she answered that they don't take money for Quran. I was both overwhelmed and surprised. I appreciated this chance, not only for me, but for the thousands of women who may have found a fee prohibitive. In this way, the path to Quran was open to all.

There were two tracks for an *ijāza*. One was a '*tajwīd ijāza*'. This meant that I would have to learn to implement and teach all the rules of *tajwīd*, memorize an ancient poem of the rules, memorize a portion of the Quran in *tajwīd*, and do at least one perfect read-through. I would then be tested on all of that. The second track was the '*hufẓ ijāza*', which included all of the above along with complete memorization. I began by focusing on the *tajwīd ijāza*. Although I had somewhat of a background in *tajwīd*, this was at a much different level and pace. I had planned on staying in Damascus for three weeks, but I kept extending my time there until it became four and a half months.

During this time, I spent every waking moment with the Quran. I met with my *tajwīd* teacher at least every other day. I understood only later, when I began teaching *tajwīd* students myself, how impressive her commitment and the amount of time she gave me and her other students was—may Allah bless her and reward her multiple times over. My task was to recite a certain number of pages that I had practiced beforehand. The practice was not random, but quite specific and taxing. First, I listened to a recording of the pages being recited by Shaikh Hudhaifi or Shaikh Basfar. Both *tajwīd* specialists had recordings that were specific to learners. After listening to the recording, I would read along with it a few times. Then I'd recite the pages myself about five times. Then I would repeat the process until I felt I could practice no more. I did this for every single page. I practiced loudly, with volume, losing myself in the concentration required to twist and turn my tongue and lips into shapes they had never formed before.

When I was ready to recite, I would walk down the main highway in the ninety-degree heat to my teacher's house and be directed to her large, air-conditioned salon. As I cooled off, I was often nervous about reciting, but that feeling quickly dissipated as I began. I was corrected and coached on the proper placement of my tongue, lips, and teeth. I spent every waking moment either reading Quran, thinking about Quran, or practicing the letters of the Quran. The sound of me practicing the letter '*ḍād*' could be heard by my roommates while I vacuumed the apartment, cooked (a little too spicy) *keema*, and donned my hijab for my next appointment. I ate, slept, lived, and breathed the Quran during those beautiful days of learning.

Beautiful Words That Filled Me

There was something so exhilarating and yet relaxing about reciting Quran out loud, it did not matter that I could not understand every word. It filled me and nourished me. And the recitation itself offered me deeper understandings.

In a class about the Quran, a teacher shared examples of how *tajwīd* gives meaning to the Quran. For example, in Surat Yūnus, *āyah* 91 refers to Pharaoh who, after a lifetime of disbelieving, declares his belief right before he and his army drown;

آلْآنَ وَقَدْ عَصَيْتَ قَبْلُ وَكُنتَ مِنَ الْمُفْسِدِينَ

{Now? And you had disobeyed before and were of the corrupters?}[3]

The timing of the first word in the verse, "*Āl'ān*" is lengthened significantly and could indicate the long time he took to finally believe, almost like saying, "Nooooooow? After all this time?"

Dr. Ingrid Mattson highlights the significance of reciting the Quran in Arabic and with *tajwīd*: "To translate the Quran to another language is to lose the powerful aural effect of the rhymes, assonance, and other harmonious and poetic aspects of the Arabic words. In addition, it is clearly impossible to reproduce the *tajwīd* of the recited Arabic Quran in a translation."[4]

Finding My 'Flow'

I did not understand much Arabic at the time, but I didn't find it difficult to recite for hours and feel the meaning through the *tajwīd* rules. Reciting Quran can be a powerful "flow activity," which is defined by Mihaly Csikszentmihalyi in his book *Flow: The Psychology of Optimal Experience* as, "The state in which people are so involved in an activity that nothing else seems to matter; the experience itself is so enjoyable that people will do it even at great cost, for the sheer sake of doing it."[5]

Csikszentmihalyi described these activities as optimal experiences during which we "feel a sense of exhilaration, a deep sense of

Flow State

enjoyment that is long cherished and that becomes a landmark in memory for what life should be like."[6] He proposed that these optimal experiences can lead to a greater sense of happiness and contentment, two goals that every human being knowingly or unknowingly yearns for. For example,

> It is what the sailor holding a tight course feels when the wind whips through her hair, when the boat lunges through the waves like a colt—sails, hull, wind, and sea humming a harmony that vibrates in the sailor's veins. It is what a painter feels when the colors on the canvas begin to set up a magnetic tension with each other, and a new thing, a living form, takes shape in front of the astonished creator. Or it is the feeling a father has when his child for the first time responds to his smile.[7]

Before we conclude that these activities are synonymous with relaxation or pleasure, Csikszentmihalyi further clarifies, "Contrary to what we usually believe, moments like these, the best moments in our lives, are not the passive, receptive, relaxing times—although such experiences can also be enjoyable, if we have worked hard to attain them. The best moments usually occur when a person's body or mind is stretched to its limits in a voluntary effort to accomplish something difficult and worthwhile. Optimal experience is thus something that we *make* happen. For a child, it could be trying to beat his own record; for a violinist, mastering an intricate musical passage."[8] I would like to add to his list reciting and memorizing Quran. It was an optimal experience for me.

Of course we know that reading Quran has great reward attached to it and has deep meaning in the realm of Islam. It is truly a blessing and a gift from Allah ﷻ that, in addition to the reward in the hereafter for this act, there can be great worldly joy in it also, with benefits of peace and contentment.

Focus with Friends

After a few weeks of staying in the apartment in Mezze, I moved to another apartment so I could be in a more intensive study environment. I was joined by twenty or thirty other girls working on the same goal, and we were relieved of household duties to be able to focus on completing a *khitma* (recitation of the entire Quran). I was to be tested by a sheikh prior to my return to the States to start medical school.

In this magical place there were people whose job it was to take care of all our needs so we could focus on the Quran. At 3:30 am a smiling woman, carrying a tray of Nescafe® and cookies, woke me for *tahajjud*. Food was provided, the house was cleaned, and the details of life were tended to so that all of us could be successful with the Quran. I formed friendships and bonds that continue today. We share hilarious and poignant memories of thirty-plus girls in one house with 1.5 bathrooms and a shower line that was two pages long. We would all stand around the dining table eating olives, cheese, yogurt, and bread—each one of us thinking about our progress and plan for the next day.

It wasn't long before we fell into set routines and became a unique family of memorizers. Everyone naturally claimed a specific spot at the table, and we all knew who to save the strawberry jam for and who had to have the pickled eggplant stuffed with walnuts and red peppers. There was the requisite "nerd" who outdid us all in her memorization, the "class clown" who came to dinner with her hijab under-piece tied around her head like a bandana, and the pre-teen girls who spent much of their time jumping onto mattresses from the loft in one of the bedrooms. One of my friends kept a journal she called *Aṣḥāb al-Kahf* (People of the Cave) in which she wrote quotes and memories from our time together. The best quote had to be from one of our friends who, after hours of memorizing, emerged from a room in the back of the house in a daze and said, "Why did Banī Isrā'īl have to be so bad? Surat al-Baqara wouldn't have been so long if it wasn't for them." We laughed and laughed. Later, I laughed again, thinking how these little jokes were so unique to our experience, and wondered at what women around the world were missing when they did not get to experience this intense challenge.

Time to be Tested

It took me about five weeks to complete my *khitma*, after which I waited to find out when my appointment with the sheikh would be. Then one day, just as I woke up to a new day of Quran, my friend and I were told that we were going to recite to the sheikh that very day. We looked like a couple of deer in headlights, and worked on being nervous for the few hours before we went. Thankfully, they had the wisdom not to have told us earlier. They didn't want our nerves to build up to such a degree that it would affect our recitation.

Anse Maha, the teacher who was taking us to this incredible appointment, was a quiet person by nature and did not utter a word to either of us the whole drive. Of course we were too nervous to make a peep ourselves. I was terrified. I was afraid that I would open my mouth and no sound would come out. Or that I would be too nervous to read, or, or, or... I imagined a number of disastrous scenarios.

We pulled up to an inconspicuous door, set in a modest building. We followed Anse Maha up a long flight of stairs that opened into a long room. On one side of the room was a soft, plush bench. On the other side was a thick curtain that hung from the high ceilings to the floor, and all along the length of the room. There was a line of women waiting ahead of us, all sitting with their Qurans open, reading to themselves. They were all Syrian women preparing to recite to the eminent Sheikh Al-Kurdi (may God surround him with mercy), who was sitting behind the curtain. Soon each set her *muṣḥaf* aside as, one by one, they responded to the voice behind the curtain. The sheikh began reciting an *āya* for each student and then waited for her to complete it by memory and continue for several pages. Some were asked questions about *tajwīd* rules or lines of poetry, or called upon to recite some more if the sheikh sensed some weakness in their recitation. Some passed and breathed a sigh of relief. Some were asked to go back and practice more.

When my turn came, the sheikh told me where to read from in the Quran. I was working on the *tajwīd ijāza*, so I was allowed to read from the *muṣḥaf* itself, though part of me could barely see it. I was paralyzed with nerves and had no idea where he wanted me to start. Anse Maha turned the pages of my *muṣḥaf* and silently indicated where I was to recite from. After reciting a portion of Surat al-Naba', the sheikh asked me to recite from Surat Maryam. At that point, I turned off the part of my brain that was nervous and recited loudly and clearly. Once I hesitated on a word, but was able to correct myself. I continued reading like I was never going to stop, until he said something that I did not hear. He made a joke which elicited a chuckle from Anse Maha, but I did not understand, as my Arabic was still so weak. And that was it. My turn was over.

I did not know what the result was, but dared not ask anyone, as now it was my friend's turn. I sat quietly, listening to her recitation and wondering about my fate. When my friend finished, we packed up our things and were headed down the stairs when Anse Maha whispered to me, "You got it." And that was it. She didn't say anything else. This short little phrase took time to register, so it didn't really hit me until three-quarters of our car ride home. My friend earned her *ijāza* as well, and she was also quiet on the way home, other than the occasional sniffle, which confirmed to me that it had been just as overwhelming for her as it was for me.

Celebrating!

We were greeted by excited faces and hugs when we got back to the apartment. In the four days I had left in Damascus, the obligatory *ijāza* party was thrown for us—complete with white robes and crowns. I was told to prepare a little talk for the party. In Arabic!

Terrified, I wrote out a page-long speech in English, and my Quran teacher was kind enough to translate it into Arabic for me. I practiced and practiced, and still, when I spoke, I stumbled over some words and struggled to make it sound natural. Anse Amena, known for her sense of humor, broke the ice by saying, "Let's hope she reads Quran better than that." As the room erupted in giggles, I giggled along, relieved that she'd brought attention to the difference between one's ability to recite Quran and her ability to read something else in Arabic. Nothing our teachers say is in vain. Even when it appears as just a joke, there is deep meaning to every word. It reminded all of us of the miracle of the Quran. It is not like reading any other book in Arabic. People who struggle to read other Arabic texts *can* read Quran.

Stage Two Begins

Getting my *ijāza* in *tajwīd* was the first step on my journey of memorizing the Quran. First, because learning correct pronunciation is imperative before memorizing, but just as importantly, because that is how I became attached to the Quran. By spending so much time reciting and working to perfect my *tajwīd*, I became addicted to the words, the light, and the beauty of the Quran. What came after was the natural next step. It wasn't even really a decision I had to make to start memorizing. It was a given. I'd heard again and again the reward of memorizing the Quran, the crowns that would be placed upon my parents' heads in the hereafter, and the hadith about being asked to recite and then ascending level after level in Heaven to the point where one had memorized in the Quran.

> Abdullah b. ʿAmr b. al-ʿĀṣ ؓ stated that the Prophet ﷺ said, "To the person with the Quran, it is said, 'Recite and ascend! Recite measuredly just as you used to recite in the world! Your station will be at the last verse you recite.'"[9]

عَنْ عَبْدِ اللَّهِ بْنِ عَمْرٍو، عَنِ النَّبِيِّ صَلَّى اللَّهُ عَلَيْهِ وَسَلَّمَ قَالَ: يُقَالُ—يَعْنِي لِصَاحِبِ الْقُرْآنِ: اقْرَأْ وَارْتَقِ وَرَتِّلْ كَمَا كُنْتَ تُرَتِّلُ فِي الدُّنْيَا، فَإِنَّ مَنْزِلَتَكَ عِنْدَ آخِرِ آيَةٍ تَقْرَأُ بِهَا

I wish I could say that it was the promise of the hadith that was the burning force that drove me to want to memorize, but it was not only that. Although the hadiths motivated and encouraged me, they were not the driving force behind my decision to memorize. I memorized the Quran out of love. After spending so much time with the Quran working on my *ijāza* in *tajwīd*, I became so attached to it that I could not get enough. I wanted to have the words of the Quran etched on my brain and heart. The hours I spent with the Quran were the most beautiful hours of my life. Reciting it brought a peace to my heart and mind like nothing else ever had. One of my friends, who felt the same way, described it as "wanting to eat the Quran." I must say, that's a pretty good description of how I felt.

I remember mentioning my newfound desire to memorize the entire Quran to my *tajwīd* teacher, who promptly told me that I would not be able to memorize because I did not know Arabic well enough. Here, of course, was one of those roadblocks. She meant well and was not trying to be a spoilsport. Perhaps she was truly concerned that I would get frustrated and that the frustration would be turned toward the Quran. In my interviews with women who memorized the Quran, I found that many of them did have naysayers. As a community, we need to stop saying you can't and start saying you can. We need to believe in our girls and women and uplift them in their quest. Good thing I have a competitive spirit that is ignited when challenged. It served me well at that point. Come to think of it, maybe that was her plan all along...

Figuring out how and when to memorize was a whole other story, because four days after I got my *ijāza* in *tajwīd* I was sitting in my medical school orientation.

It was exciting to finally be starting med school, after all those years of working to get in. But my free time was now filled with anatomy lab, exams every Monday (which really left no room to enjoy the weekend) and "bugs and drugs," as they say.

They also say that medical school is like trying to get a sip of water from a fire hydrant. And it is true. The fire hydrant was in full force and I was in awe of everything I was learning. I remember marveling at the perfect symmetrical alignment of the internal and external intercostal muscles in anatomy lab, being amazed at the precise compensating mechanisms of the endocrine system, and learning how to do a good physical exam. I made the decision that I would never ski down hills beyond my beginner's ability again when I realized how strong and yet delicate the human body was. All sorts of doctor things were changing me.

Throughout this whirlwind of medical habits and learning, my thoughts often went back to the Quran. I was still reading a portion of it every morning, but my wish to memorize remained as a burning spark of energy sitting and waiting to be fanned into life.

My first and only vacation was one month in the summer between my first and second years of med school. I went back to Syria and back to the memorization house. But the time was just too short and I was not able to start memorizing. Upon my return, I found a local teacher. She was a *ḥāfiẓa* and had studied with many of the same teachers that I had studied with. I had lost a full year, but in the second year of med school I began to memorize in East Lansing, Michigan. It was a far cry from the dedicated environment I had begun in, but my heart needed this memorization, so I soldiered forth. I worked on memorizing Surat al-Baqara that year, meeting with my teacher either every week or every other week. There were times when those weeks stretched into months—my exam schedule and her availability often tried to discourage me, but by the end of the year, I had completed memorizing Surat al-Baqara. I was thrilled and could see my way forward. I wanted to continue and began to plan how I might become a *ḥāfiẓa*.

I had a friend a few years my senior who had taken a year off medical school after completing her second year to travel to Egypt and learn Arabic. I began to wonder if that was something that I could do. Why not? I thought. I broached the topic with my mother, who initially hesitated, and so I dropped it in deference to her opinion. Then one day, out of nowhere, she asked me if I really was serious about wanting to memorize the Quran. That was all I needed.

The *riḍā* (gratification) of parents is an important part of memorizing Quran. I knew that I needed it for *tawfīq* (serendipitous blessing) in any undertaking, and especially this one. I didn't look back. I focused on finishing the rest of my second year of medical school and taking my first board exam. Two weeks after I answered the last question on that test, I was on a plane back to Syria.

The Year of Memorization

As the plane started its descent through the night sky, I was barely able to make out the familiar rooftops of houses in little villages dotting the brown landscape. The scenery was the same, but I was different. My first trip had opened my eyes and awakened something in my heart and mind that made it clear I could never go back to "before." This time when I got off the plane, it was different. This time,

I had a clear purpose and goal in my mind, and I was determined. I was not going to leave until I achieved what I had set out to do.

My year there started out with the summer program for Americans that I had attended twice already. At the end of the program, most of the girls left. The few who remained slowly trickled out as their departure dates approached. As the American girls were leaving, Syrian college students slowly started filling up the house. During the year, the house was used as a dorm for girls who lived in the cities outside of Damascus. Pretty soon, all my friends were gone and I was the only English-speaking person left.

My drive and conviction were my friends during this time. I threw myself into my goal and got started as soon as possible. I was assigned a new teacher who was one of the best. It's interesting how teachers and students were paired up. Every person needed a specific kind of teacher, and it still leaves me in awe how perfect the pairings were... most of the time (more to come on this later). For example, when it came to Quran (and I suppose most things in life), I just put my mind to it, blocked out anything that could be an obstacle, and did it. I was sent a teacher who was exactly like that, but even more so. She had razor sharp focus. During our lessons, we started out with a little small talk, but not too much. We didn't get into each other's lives or business much, which was just fine for the introvert in me; I had other teachers who guided me in life matters. In addition, her *tajwīd* was impeccable. I was in awe of how crisp and clear and strong her letter *rā* was. Some of my other friends had Quran teachers who took them deeper on a personal journey of spiritual upbringing and built a relationship with them outside of recitation. But this was a perfect setup for me. I had a goal, and I was going to focus and get it done.

And so my journey started. I began with Surat al-Baqara, although I had already memorized it in America. I prepared five pages at a time and then called my teacher to schedule an appointment. I used to hop on a micro-bus, which was usually packed with people on their way to work, school, social visits, and other life adventures, and ride to a nearby neighborhood, get off and then walk past a pizza place with a life-size cut-out of a large, happy man with a curly mustache serving pizza. I was always looking for that large happy man with the curly mustache so that I would make the correct corner turn and find the gray building I was looking for. Most of the buildings were block buildings with flats—a leftover architectural idiosyncrasy that spanned both the colonial period and socialism—and the buildings all looked the same. So, I needed that pizza guy. At Anse Rida's building, I would open the heavy iron doors and enter the cooler air of shade and cement. Three flights of stairs, a knock on the wooden door, and I had arrived. The door would swing wide and there would be a large welcoming smile that belonged to either my teacher, her mother, or her sister. Then I would be ushered into the salon—a room with intricately decorated mother-of-pearl furniture and an embroidered wall hanging reminiscent of the Victorian era. I loved having this time to quickly do a last read-through of the pages I was going to recite.

Although my teacher was a no-nonsense kind of person, she was very kind and would always enter with a smile and chit chat a bit about neutral, suitable-for-introvert topics before beginning our recitation session. I would go through my five pages, and she would mark any mistakes I made in my *muṣḥaf*. Afterwards, she would tell me if the pages were acceptable or not. Most of the time they were, *al-ḥamdu lillāh*.

And so the days went on. At the same time, I enrolled in Arabic classes at the University of Damascus that I attended from 9:00 am to 1:00 pm every day except Friday. I would come home after Arabic class and sit down to memorize Quran for the next four hours. The evening would usually be spent with dinner, socializing with the others in the dorm, and quickly getting through my Arabic homework.

My personal method for memorizing was not that complicated. I usually memorized one verse at a time and would then put the ones I'd memorized together. Once I could recite an entire page orally and without hesitation or mistake, I would use the litmus test that Anse Tamara had advised me to use when I started memorizing. Quoting the Prophet ﷺ, who said, "Tie up knowledge by writing,"[10]

عن أنس أنه قال: قال النبي صلى الله عليه وسلم: **قَيِّدُوا العِلْمَ بِالكِتَاب**

she advised me to write the verses without checking back, once I thought I knew them. If I could write out the whole page from memory, then I would go on to the next page. Once I had collected five pages, I would practice them until I could recite all five well. Then I would be off to my teacher's house again, past the happy pizza man, up the stairs, and into the room with the pearl furniture. I usually went twice a week with five pages. I did this throughout the year.

And what a beautiful year it was. It was not an easy year; I worked hard, I got homesick, and I struggled to understand the Syrian dialect. But I had found my flow, was in an "optimal experience," and was moving steadily forward. There was only one time I got stuck in my memorization.

The Day I Got Stuck

Anse Tamara told me her own story of getting stuck. She would go at six in the morning to her Quran teacher and recite. This one particular morning, she was reciting and came to verses about hajj and for some reason could not remember them. Her teacher asked her, "Did you recite to yourself with a recorder?"

"Yes."

"Did you write it down without looking?"

"Yes."

So she sent Anse Tamara to the other room to review. She said that she went back three times to her teacher and still couldn't recite those verses! So finally she said, "Ok *yā* Rabb! I intend to go on Hajj!" She had not yet been to hajj, and had no money for hajj, and had young children and no one to leave them with, but the minute she made that intention—she was able to complete the page. She told me, "I wasn't able to memorize the verses because I had not intended hajj. It didn't matter that I couldn't go based on my circumstances—I needed to intend to do my *farḍ*. And, *al-ḥamdu lillāh,* when I figured that out, the pages became easy." I learned from this story to be on the lookout for any verses that were inexplicably difficult to memorize. Certainly, the entire process took time, hard work, and focus, but I did not struggle with any particular *āya* until I got toward the end, when I came to an *āya* that touched upon an issue I had been struggling with all year. When it came time to recite that *āya* to my Quran teacher, I found that I was unable to do it. It just would not come out of my mouth. I tried, I stumbled, I stopped. I tried again...

I stumbled, I got flustered... and finally, I asked my teacher if I could just stop for that day and come back again in a few days. I went home and reflected. I made *du'ā'* that Allah ﷻ would help me overcome this barrier. I searched the page that I could not recite to see which part exactly I was having difficulty with. When I came upon the *āya*, {And We have already created man and know what his soul whispers to him, and We are closer to him than [his] jugular vein,}[11] I knew that was it. The answer was there. Allah ﷻ is the One Who created me and He knows my deepest thoughts. And He provided the answer in diagramming out how close He is to us. In fact, my mind could not help but picture a Frank Netter anatomy textbook drawing of the jugular vein and remember how its purpose is to bring blood back to the heart. I took a deep breath and repeated the *āya* over and over again until I felt it sinking in to my heart.

When I went back, I took a few deep breaths and started again. This time, *al-ḥamdu lillāh*, I made it through. My struggle was with submission. I was struggling to turn off the intellectual and analytical portion of my brain that caused me to overthink things. I was struggling with letting go, submitting, and going with the ebb and flow of life.

Neuroplasticity and the Quran

Many years later, I developed an interest in learning more about neuroplasticity and the ability of the brain to rewire connections to heal physical injuries or change habits. What I found was so fascinating and, looking back, I could relate it to not only this situation, but so many aspects of memorizing Quran. One of the foremost names in the field of neuroplasticity, Norman Doige, says that "The brain can be improved so that we learn and perceive with greater precision, speed, and retention."[12] He also claims that we can change the very structure of the brain itself and increase its capacity to learn. "Unlike a computer, the brain is constantly adapting itself."[13] He used his research to design many different programs for people, such as one for cognitively-impaired people which improves their cognitive performance after only thirty to sixty hours of treatment. His basic argument is that "practicing a new skill, under the right conditions, can change hundreds of millions and possibly billions of the connections between the nerve cells in our brain maps."[14] One aspect of this change in neuronal connections is repetition. Doige says the cerebral cortex, the thin outer layer of the brain, "...is actually selectively refining its processing capacities to fit each task at hand. It doesn't simply learn; it is always 'learning how to learn.'"[15]

The concept of neuroplasticity also gives hope to people who do not believe they have a good memory. Neuroscientist Eleanor Maguire conducted a study on mental athletes who had done well in the World Memory Championship. The mental athletes and matched control subjects were asked to memorize three-digit numbers, photographs of faces, and magnified images of snowflakes while their brains were being scanned in an MRI scanner. They found no structural differences between the two sets of brains, but what they did find was that when they looked at which parts of the brain were lighting up while the mental athletes were memorizing, they were activating entirely different circuitry. The regions of the brain that were less active in the control subjects were working in overdrive for the mental athletes.[16]

Another phenomenon I noticed is that there are some *āyāt* that are just difficult for many people. For example, there are three pages in Surat al-Baqara that are about divorce and the rulings involving it. I struggled with those pages, and that struggle made me look deeper into the meanings of the verses.

When I was ready to recite the verses of divorce, I felt such a sense of relief and lightness as I made my way to my teacher's house. I was thinking, "Thank Allah those pages of divorce are behind me." At that moment, I paused and realized that my relief was probably 1% of what someone who had gone through a divorce and moved on must have felt—"Thank Allah that's behind me." The act of memorizing the verses of Quran in and of itself became my teacher again and again. When you repeat the verses of Quran over and over again, struggling to make them stick, you notice patterns and words you may not have noticed before. Life lessons come alive on this journey. When I noticed the repetition of the same or similar phrases in different places of the Quran, I knew I would have to make a conscious effort not to drift off into the wrong sura after reciting an oft-repeated verse. Likewise, in life, we need to ensure that similar situations do not send us into unconscious habits, but that we live life intentionally. My struggle to memorize opened doors of personal meaning and rich understandings; it gave me a new relationship with the Quran and my faith.

Getting Comfortable

As the year went on, I also settled down in Damascus in a way that felt more like home. I not only got used to the food, but I had picked out my favorite dishes. I looked forward to seeing *ma'lūbe*, a dish that looks like a Bundt® cake but is made of rice and fried eggplant, *ṣfīḥa,* cheese or meat pies, and *ūzi*, round filo dough shells filled with rice, peas, meat, and nuts and served with yogurt for dipping. I also contributed to cooking for the dorm girls once every two weeks. Knowing my spice tolerance would be different than theirs, I tried to find dishes that resembled some of their Syrian ones. I usually settled for a sort of *kabsa*, rice cooked in a base of tomato sauce and spices, into which I snuck some of my own biryani spices.

What really cemented my place in the dorm and made me stop feeling like a guest was joining in on spring cleaning. Because Syria is so dusty, a couple of times in the year, a deep cleaning of every nook and cranny is required. On my previous trip, we hadn't participated in this ritual, as we were only there for a short time, and our teachers wanted us to focus on our studies. But this time, I joined in as we took buckets of water mixed with laundry detergent, dipped big rags inside, and used them to wash over every cabinet, wall, and sofa. Cleaning is a great activity for anyone on a spiritual path—the analogies are endless, and you can preoccupy your mind with thoughts of cleaning your heart while your hands are scrubbing up the hidden crevices of dirt in the corners of the closet. The carpet was like the heart of the room. No matter how beautiful and shiny the rest of the room looked, if the carpet was dusty, it brought the whole room down. We kept it vacuumed and wiped, but during spring cleaning, it got beaten and scrubbed. I remember thinking that the heart is like this—we need daily clean-ups and seasonal deep cleans in order to stay spiritually healthy.

One time, we were so behind in our cleaning that we didn't have time to clean the ceiling fan before the head of the dorm came to inspect. "It doesn't matter," we said, "She won't notice." As she went from room to room, we waited, quite proud of our efforts. Then she entered the salon and immediately enquired. "Why didn't you clean the fan?" We tried to fit that into our analogies as well, and decided it fit in with realizing the importance of attention to detail when it comes to cleaning out our inner selves. Not letting things slide, thinking they are small and unimportant. Sometimes we would spend so much time cleaning a sofa, wiping off the dust from every crevice, and making the velvet seats shimmer by scrubbing them down with soap and water, only to move the sofa to reveal an even bigger mess of dust and fallen pencils behind it. We realized that we could have ignored the garbage behind the sofa. After all, no one would see it. But, eventually, it would grow and expand so much that it would spill out from the sides and spread particles of dust all over the room. All that dust and junk made us all think about the diseases of the heart we were learning about and how they needed similar time and meticulous attention. After all, a sound heart will be one of the most valuable things in the hereafter as described in some of my favorite verses.

يَوْمَ لَا يَنفَعُ مَالٌ وَلَا بَنُونَ

إِلَّا مَنْ أَتَى اللَّهَ بِقَلْبٍ سَلِيمٍ

The day when there will not benefit [anyone] wealth nor children
But only one who comes to Allah with a sound heart."[17]

By that time, I was sometimes memorizing more than five pages at a time. I wanted to make it through my first complete memorization before I left, although I found the last part of the Quran harder to memorize due to the shorter verses. Many people find the chapters with shorter *āyāt* easier to memorize, but I liked the longer *āyāt* because I could memorize an entire page by only having to memorize the beginnings of two or three *āyāt*. Many people, including myself, memorize each verse separately first and then put them together to connect the whole page. Once you know the verses well, all you need to recite it almost without thinking is the trigger of the first few words. The fewer verses there are on a page, the fewer beginnings you need to remember.

And Then It Was None

After a whole year of working so hard to memorize and thinking the end would be so exciting, it was ironic how anti-climactic my last day ended up being. I worked until the day before I left and even recited the last few chapters of *Juzu' 'Amma* in my Quran teacher's car as she drove me to a market so I could do some last-minute shopping.

My teacher was very balanced in her emotions—not one to get too happy or too sad. When I recited Surat al-Nās and then went back to recite Surat al-Fātiḥa and the first page of Surat al-Baqara, she turned to me with an ever-so-slight smile and said, "*Mabrūk*"—congratulations. She handed me a little pad of stationary with a pen as a gift. We parted ways there in that little market place. I was a new *ḥāfiẓa,* and I was headed back to medical school. In hindsight, I'm glad it was an understated end, because what came after was going to be an even a greater challenge.

Carrying the Quran

The first and only thing that the mentor who oversaw us at the boarding house said to me about my completion of my first *khitma* was, "*Mashallah mabrūk*—congratulations. Now you must go out and be with people so that it was not all for yourself. You have to give them light."

Memorizing the Quran in a year needed focus and a distraction-free environment. Even when I wasn't actively memorizing, it was always on my mind. I'd been similarly focused in medical school. Back in those days, I'd had a hard time switching from the intensity required for studying to the looser mindset required when I was attempting to relax. Making that transition was difficult for me, and I was not very good at living in the moment. My mentor recognized that in me and, essentially, she was telling me I needed to do it better. "When you're with people, actually be *with* them." It was important advice, but it took me a while to learn how to do it.

Her words were beautiful for more than one reason. She didn't tell me, "Now go preach to people." She said simply, "BE with people." There are so many layers to that seemingly small bit of wisdom. While there is a time and place to teach people what one has learned, most of what we "teach" is silent. When you memorize the Quran, you carry it in your heart, and it is always there as an active participant in every interaction. It silently seeps into those around you. Sometimes they might feel a certain sense of peace around you, without quite being able to pinpoint its source. Other times, it might manifest as an inner strength or solidity of faith they detect in you.

When I had gotten my *ijāza* in *tajwīd* and returned immediately to my first year of medical school, one of our icebreakers at orientation had consisted of forming small groups and writing on cards one thing we wanted to take from each person and one thing we wanted to give them during our time together in medical school. More than one person wrote on my card that they wanted to take from me my sense of peace. They could sense it upon meeting me—and they were not even Muslims. Of course, after that, my inner tranquility waxed and waned, but at that time it was a dominant part of me. I've since realized that it is something that needs to be nurtured and protected. The more I keep up with reviewing Quran, the stronger this part of me becomes. But it is a gift that can go as quickly as it comes.

One thing that helped was to remember one of the mantras of my teachers, that the night is for Allah ﷻ and the day is for work. The pre-Fajr time is when one has a good 'spiritual breakfast' to last throughout the day. I was blessed in Damascus to be studying Quran and Arabic during the day, although of course that wouldn't always be the case in normal, everyday life. I would have to make a concerted effort to ensure that I did my Quran reading/reviewing in the morning, before the demands of the day crowded in. Because the rest of the day is for going to school/work and spending time with family, friends, and students.

The other parting words I received after completing my first *khitma* and before returning to the United States were from a special teacher of great spiritual stature, whom I visited to say goodbye. I was escorted into the room and sat in front of her to hear her parting words. She congratulated me and then asked a question that left me speechless. "Can you feel it dancing around in your heart?"

It wasn't something I had ever talked about to anyone, but yes, I could feel it dancing around in my heart. I could physically feel the Quran in my heart. I never expected that. Muslims often speak of people who have memorized the Quran as 'carriers of the Quran.' But after having done it, I realized it was meant quite literally. I felt like I was carrying it around with me.

She gave me a few more words of advice, encouraged me to make sure that I always taught people, and with that I was set to sail. I treasure those words and often look back at them for strength and solace.

Stage Three: Struggles

I faced other challenges upon my return. I went from putting hijab on at the age of twenty-one to having memorized the entire Quran by the age of twenty-six. I was not ready to be called '*ḥāfiẓa*' or hailed as a person of great spiritual stature, because I didn't consider myself either. At most, I accepted to call myself "someone who has memorized the Quran once" or "someone who completed a *khitma 'al-ghaib* once." To me, a *ḥāfiẓ/ḥāfiẓa* was someone who could lead *tarāwīḥ* or recite from anywhere in the Quran, anytime and anyplace, from memory. And I certainly did not see myself as someone who was spiritually elevated or worthy (or able) to guide people on a spiritual path. The most I allowed myself to do was teach *tajwīd*.

Although many of my teachers were *ḥāfiẓāt*, their stature felt out of reach to me. I felt guilty that I was not as perfect as I thought someone who memorized the Quran should be. I felt like an imposter. I wasn't someone who grew up reading Quran all the time. Although my family had religion in the house, we were not a family of scholars or *ḥuffāẓ*.

My path was not one that was expected of me. There were other things expected of me, like doing well in school, getting a good degree, and walking the same path that most women are expected to take. I did some of those things. But in my family, in my community, and amongst the larger family of American-Muslim women, I was an anomaly. I was making my own path, and it was scary at times.

I often felt alone. Especially after having been so focused on my memorizing and surrounded by other young women who were also working on the same goal. After I came home, I struggled with this for many years, especially because I really had to tap into my internal motivation.

Now, although I have increased in knowledge and maturity, I still don't see myself where I would hope to be in many ways, including my review of Quran memorization. However, I see every stage in the path as a necessary stepping stone. I realized that, by shying away from my accomplishment, I had been making the same mistake that is made by people who question whether or not they should wear hijab—avoiding a good deed because they are not perfect in other ways. The same goes for any act of religious devotion. We allow ourselves to get deterred from doing good because we are not good *enough*. If we say that out loud, it sounds absurd. And yet we do it. It is one of Satan's favorite tricks to steer someone off the path who cannot be tricked with other transgressions. We all have different strengths and weaknesses. We are all striving in one way or another.

Eventually, what broke me out of this negative way of thinking was realizing that it was not up to me to decide what Allah ﷻ gives me. Who was I to question Allah's ﷻ choice of my path? Memorizing was certainly never something I dreamed I would do, but I realized I had to seize the gift, cherish it, and own it. Allah ﷻ does not make mistakes. There is a reason for everything, whether we understand it or not. I draw strength from repeating to myself the *āya*, {Oh Yaḥyā, take this book with strength}[18] as I see myself owning my blessings.

There were other reasons I shied away from announcing my accomplishment. I had this idea that, unless there was a specific reason for people to know, why should I 'brag' about it? My goal was to have the Quran shine through in my character and good deeds. Perhaps people would see something good in me and wonder where it came from. I hoped that if they somehow found out after the fact, they would be able to say, "Aha! That's it!"

Time to Share

After all these years, though, I see the importance of encouraging other people to move forward in their own relationship with the Quran, whether that means learning *tajwīd*, studying the exegesis of the Quran, or working on memorizing. I didn't have a lot of female role models ahead of me in this path, but it became time for me to be one.

For a long time, I hesitated to give people advice on how to memorize Quran because I had taken a year off from medical school to travel abroad and did it there. Most people cannot do that. But, what I forgot was that I did not start memorizing in Damascus. I started in my second year of medical school. That year, along with the hours of studying I had to do to pass all my classes *and* the Step 1 exams, I took out a little time every morning to work on memorizing Surat al-Baqara. And *al-ḥamdu lillāh*, I did it. Sometimes doors open for us because of the effort we put in when we assume we do not have the time to do something. Just like the people who swear that, if they were millionaires, they would spend in the path of Allah ﷻ but do not spend when they are thousandaires. The same is true of time. You may not have the most ideal situation time-wise, but if you really want to, you can find five minutes a day to devote to something you care about. Based on your intention and effort, bigger doors may open. But you can only know if you put in the initial effort.

As far as how it changed me, I wish I could say it made me a perfect person. But unfortunately, there is no magic pill to suddenly wake up perfect—even memorizing the Quran. Memorizing does help one stay anchored to her faith through the ups and downs of life, but the real hard work of refining one's character and becoming a person who embodies the character of the Prophet ﷺ is just that. Hard work. And then there was the hard lesson to learn—that perfect is not human, it is divine. In the end, it is our character that matters and our effort. Our worship is a means to help us attain that end. I could self-identify as a *ḥāfiẓa* as soon as I realized that perfection was an unattainable goal. I did not have to embody the image of perfection I held in my head; instead, I had to share my dancing heart with the hearts that yearned to dance.

Memorizing the Quran gave me a heightened awareness of myself and where I needed to be going. It made me want to constantly learn more about the meanings of the Quran and try to live up to them. It honed my spiritual senses and gave my heart the sensitivity to quiver at questionable situations, people, or places. It gave me a sense of closeness to Allah ﷻ. I can see that, anytime I start veering off the path, Allah ﷻ pulls me back in and lovingly accepts me back into His embrace.

In fact, the Quran can become one's most reliable barometer when it comes to self-reflection and self-improvement. I know now that if I am struggling with my reviewing, I need to look at my life and see if there is something I am doing wrong. Am I transgressing someone's rights? Am I listening to things I should not be listening to? Usually, with a little reflection, it becomes quite clear what one needs to work on. My teacher always said, "It is usually that first thing that pops into your mind that you keep pushing to the side, saying, 'No, it's not that.' Usually, it is exactly that."

Review and Renew

Another new challenge was (and still is) trying to fit in reviewing Quran regularly. Life happens. Real life happens. There is school, and work, and family, and community work. For some reason, I found that reviewing has been exponentially harder than memorizing the first time around. Part of that may be because there is a unique kind of excitement and motivation the first time around. There is also the clear-cut goal of making it to the end. I have heard others say the same thing as well. The best way to do it is to be consistent, even if it's a little. That is sometimes easier said than done, but it is still a good goal to keep. I've struggled with this a great deal over the years. There are times when I've been on a roll, and there are times when I've 'fallen off the wagon.' While you can find memorizing Quran enjoyable, especially when you have built up momentum and are 'on a roll', there will be days where you struggle to sit down and get started. I was recently listening to an audiobook, *The Confidence Gap*, which provided a good method for urging yourself to do something when you do not feel like it. The key word is 'feel.' If we choose to do or not do things based on how we feel, we may never do the things we should do or need to do. Rather, we should act based on our values.[19] Once we know our values, and we put memorizing Quran on that list, then choosing to act on our values over our feelings will help us to push through on those difficult days. Often, I find it is starting that is the greatest challenge. But if I can stick to my values and get over the milestone of starting, my feelings often follow and I can get into it. The times I've done the best were when I had a teacher to recite to regularly—and the closer the teacher lived, the more consistent I could remain. In my review life, I have started over many times due to having to find new teachers.

I used to make yearly trips to Syria, even if for two or three weeks and, during that time, I started my *sabr*. *Sabr* is the process of review that one must undertake to get her *ijāza 'al-ghaib* or the *ijāza* that bears witness to impeccable *tajwīd* and memorization. It entails being able to recite five *ajzā'* of the Quran at a time. Once I had the five parts down pat, I would be tested by a senior *tajwīd* specialist, in my case Dr. Hadia, who started reciting an *āya* and then stopped and asked me to complete it. This was done for every five *ajzā'* throughout the whole Quran. Once I had completed the Quran again, and been tested on each set of five *ajzā'*, I would move on to ten *ajzā'* together. It is quite a feat to hold ten parts of the Quran in your mind and heart, and a greater one when it is the entire Quran. I remember my first tests with Dr. Hadia. First, she could tell immediately that I was not reciting all the pages in my prayer. And, second, the mistakes she corrected me on, I will never forget. Those are etched in my mind forever. Every time I read the first page of Surat al-Nisā' and the phrase '*fa-l-yasta'fif*,' I am immediately transported back to Dr. Hadia's salon and can picture her correcting my letter '*fa*.' I got a good start during these two or three-week trips, but I was unable to complete my *sabr* in Syria. I continue to work on it today in the USA.

It is frustrating to make it to a certain point and then be interrupted because you or your teacher move away. But I have learned an important lesson from so many starts without corresponding finishes. The end result is important, but equally important is the time and effort we put into it, no matter where it may lead. Any moment we spend with the Quran holds great weight. I know I not only got the reward for all those hours of practicing, but each time I have to re-do a section, it stays with me more and is carved more deeply on my heart. And then there are the unseen spiritual benefits. There is the washing away of sin that comes with worship. '...for, verily, good deeds drive away evil deeds...'[20] There is grounding that comes from spending time with the Quran. There is connection with Allah ﷻ. It is not time lost. There is only gain.

Time to Teach

In addition to reviewing for memorization, I make sure that the person I am reciting to corrects my *tajwīd*. An interesting phenomenon in the world of *tajwīd* is that getting an *ijāza* in *tajwīd* does not mean that you will always have perfect *tajwīd*. Just like memorizing the Quran, it is a lifelong commitment. A good way to do it is to keep reciting to a teacher who can nudge you here and there to keep your *tajwīd* straight. And to teach *tajwīd* is the very best method of review and practice. In fact, on the *ijāza* certificate itself, it is written that the holder cannot turn people away who seek to learn Quran from her. I make sure that I always have at least one student that I am teaching *tajwīd* to so I can uphold the *amāna* (trust) of the *ijāza* and it does not just become a piece of paper hanging on the wall.

Chapter Two
The Women Who Could

"Write what should not be forgotten."
Isabel Allende

After writing my own story, it occurred to me that many women would not be able to relate to my experience. I was lucky to be able to take time off after having started medical school and go abroad to focus on learning the Quran and Arabic. Not everyone is able to do that. Moreover, people might feel like they are 'too old' to do it now, or they are too busy with multiple children, household duties, or a full-time job. Some women experience the challenge of 'mommy brain' after having children, which causes them to question their ability to memorize anything. Professional women's days are filled outside and they come home exhausted in the evenings.

I decided to pre-emptively address some of these concerns and fears by interviewing other women who had also memorized the Quran. Women whose stories were different than mine. I wanted to find women with a variety of ages, life situations, and cultural backgrounds. The message I want to be able to impart was that memorizing the Quran is not for a select few. It is not only for Arabs; it is not only for those who memorized it before a certain age. And there is no such thing as 'it is over for me.' Whether you are able to go abroad or not, whether you have children or not, whether you are young or young at heart, whether your career is demanding or not, whether you think you have a good memory or not. The Quran is for you and you can be one of those blessed to carry it in your heart.

Women need to be able to see themselves as *ḥāfiẓāt*. This was the other motivation for me to reach out to women memorizers and write this book: none of the women I knew personally who had memorized had ever shared their stories. I am not sure why we as women do not feel comfortable sharing our stories, and I am sure it is multi-factorial.

The other day I was listening to a TED talk by Reshma Saujani during my morning commute. The talk was entitled, 'Teach girls bravery, not perfection.' Her words hit me like a ton of bricks. She cited research showing that girls tend to strive for perfection at the cost of trying a new task, while boys are willing to put themselves out there no matter what. This phenomenon holds girls back from achieving in many areas and fields.[21]

Indeed, many of the women I interviewed had the underlying feeling that they were not worthy of the title of *ḥāfiẓa*. They felt they needed to know the Quran better before they could claim it. I have had those same feelings myself. In fact, I had to battle these feelings and thoughts when embarking on writing this book, and it took me many years and much encouragement to begin the process. I did not think I was the right person to write about memorizing the Quran, as I know many women whose memorization is more solid than mine. It was these feelings that kept me and others from sharing our stories, and it is them that I hope to overcome through these stories, so that we can encourage other women to deepen their relationship with the Quran.

Marian Wright Edelman says, "You can't be what you can't see."[22] When I realized that I may be held accountable in the hereafter for not sharing my story and hopefully igniting a spark in others for the Quran, I shuddered. I imagined the hadith, "Recite and ascend." What if all the women who ascend to the highest level because of memorizing the whole Quran will be asked by women who do not make it as far, "Why didn't you tell me? Why didn't you hold my hand and take me along this path with you? You knew and you didn't share."

It is frightening to think that I was given this valuable thing and I have not shared the gift with others. I think back to my own childhood and the examples of women I knew who had memorized the Quran, and I can count them on one finger. It was not until my college years that I heard of another. And I certainly did not hear either of their stories or get much in the way of encouragement. Even though I knew they had memorized the Quran, I did not know how, or when, or why, or any details that might have encouraged me to follow in their gentle footsteps.

A recurring theme in my interviews of modern women who have memorized the Quran was a feeling of embarrassment. Instead of healthy pride and joyous thankfulness, women were afraid of being labeled or stigmatized. The fear of being placed in a box or becoming a one-dimensional character in the eyes of others was palpable. Some of the women voiced fears of telling people because "it was the nerdy thing to do" or "they'll think I can't laugh or be normal anymore."

The thing is, memorizing Quran does not make anyone a one-dimensional character. It does not transform one's personality or mean that she must stop laughing and be serious all the time. It does not limit her career choices or prevent her from being a stay-at-home mom. Memorizing the Quran is only one aspect of our human self. It is meant to beautify us as people, strengthen us, and give us a beautiful, solid foundation from which to use the rest of our talents and gifts to serve humanity.

Women are often discouraged from memorizing the Quran for reasons ranging from "You'll get your period and won't be able to review enough," to "What's the point of women memorizing since they don't lead *tarāwīḥ*?" While these comments may seem harmless and unworthy of mention, I heard some stories of women who were memorizing the Quran and stopped because of these kinds of words. Two of their stories are told in Chapter Five, 'The Stories That Weren't.' It was a painful chapter to write, but it's important that we hear those stories as well.

I interviewed women from a wide variety of backgrounds, ages, and life stages, including Americans of Pakistani and Syrian descent, converts, white Americans and black Americans, one woman who was born and raised in Sudan, and two women who were born and raised in Syria. Most of them are currently living in the US. Some of them memorized the Quran before getting married and having children, while some did it afterwards. Some were working outside the home in their respective fields, while some put their careers on hold after having children and were home most of the day with them.

Despite the differences in demographics of these women, there were a few recurring themes in their interviews. First, for most of them, it was not modesty that prevented them from sharing that they had memorized the Quran, but a lack of confidence. They felt they wanted to perfect it more before telling people. Some did not want people's perceptions of them to change, afraid they would be seen as stodgy and overly religious. They all expressed in some way or another that memorizing the Quran deepened their faith and drew them into a closer relationship with Allah ﷻ, but many of them expressed concern about keeping up with reviewing. But they all said they would choose to do it again.

Many of the women felt a spiritual growth, almost like the Quran and the process of memorizing it was their teacher. It was not only rote memorization, but rather a dynamic process. The ups and downs they faced throughout their journeys taught them patience, gratitude, persistence and humility. Many of them also stressed the role that *tarbiya* (spiritual upbringing) from a teacher played in their process. For some it was their Quran teacher, while for others it was another teacher. Their teachers helped them navigate the roadblocks and see the wisdom in times of ease.

Many of them had similar methods for memorizing, but some had their own unique methods. One thing that they all agreed upon as the number one prerequisite to memorizing the Quran, though, was intention. They kept coming back to that again and again. They also all agreed that repetition was important no matter what kind of schedule they used.

The women differed in that a few of them grew up surrounded by Quran and saw female role models early on who had memorized. They also had access to teachers from a young age and had embarked on the journey as young children. However, for many of them, it was not something they even thought of until much later in life because they had never come across any *ḥāfiẓāt*. They were just never exposed to the idea.

The stories of my sisters in memorization are inspiring and motivating. Their crowning ventures become a shared journey in the coming pages as they tell their stories in their own voices. There are similarities and differences to be sure, but each woman has her own love, her own energy, and her own hopes for her sisters in faith.

Chapter Three
Women of Quran

"The Quran is a banquet from God, so take as much of it as you can."
Abdullah b. Mas'ūd

1. Charlotte

Charlotte was sixty-six years old when I had the honor of interviewing her and was just as much in love with the Quran as she had been at the age of twenty-eight, when she converted to Islam. Born and raised in Atlanta, Georgia, she converted in 1978 when she attended an Eid gathering with her then-husband. She hadn't heard much about Islam, but her heart was moved to accept it.

She was going through a difficult time in her life, and she used to listen to the Quran a great deal. "The first suras I listened to were al-Ḍuḥā and al-Inshirāḥ. I was just so moved by what Allah ﷻ was saying in those two chapters that it was like light in the middle of the night, and it brought so much peace to my heart." The same sheikh who had presided over her conversion had been teaching her about Islam. She called him to ask about these two chapters of the Quran, and he picked up the phone on the first ring. She asked to hear him recite them and to give her a little explanation about their significance. He did and, from that point on, she was attached to the Quran.

Charlotte memorized her first *juzu'* just by listening to the verses over and over again. "Of course I had to go back and learn the alphabet after that, but it was beautiful to me. I loved it so much. From the beginning, it spoke to my heart." After memorizing her first pages without any knowledge of Arabic letters, and only through imitation of the sounds, Charlotte began to find ways to learn how to read, or at least phonetically decode, the Quran in Arabic. "It was very difficult back then, of course, being a black woman and trying to learn Quran. "There were no females to teach me, so even with the alphabet I had to just get as much as I could from wherever I could, speaking to different Arab sisters and asking them, 'Well, how do you say this letter?' Or 'How do you say this? Say this line for me.'"

Many of the women Charlotte reached out to just did not have the skills to help her. They were willing, but many were illiterate in Arabic, or just did not have the background in the necessary Quranic sciences to provide her with tutelage. She reached out to the men, but they did not take her seriously. "...Trying to get it from the brothers, I had to practically beg for it. I was deemed crazy. 'Oh, that's that woman trying to learn Quran? She's crazy.'" She struggled to learn basic reading skills, but did not stop memorizing.

Charlotte found one person willing to help her, but he soon went back to Saudi Arabia and Charlotte was at a standstill. She did not give up, however, and finally found another person who agreed to listen to her recite. Her new Quran instructor, however, did not have classes for women, and would not make himself available to her in person. His solution was to listen to her recitation on the phone. She used to call her teacher every morning at 7:30 am to recite the pages she had memorized overnight. Her days were spent working full time to support herself, coming home and memorizing through the night, fitting in sleep and food as she could, and then reciting on her way to start another day.

Her mosque had two imams. One was from Sudan and the other from Syria. Both were in awe of her ability to memorize, but neither made it easy for her. When, finally, one of them agreed to teach her, he, too, fell under scrutiny and criticism from community members. Her tenacity and resolve were trialed again and again, but she remained determined and grateful for every accomplishment.

During her days of memorization and recitation, her imam made sure that her Quran was correct. "If I made a mistake, he would tell me, 'No, you go fix it.'" He was neither gentle nor sensitive to her feelings. He did not couch his criticism in pretty words or gentle phrases. And he did not leave her in error with the excuse that she was a woman or a non-Arab. Many times Charlotte felt that he had been quite mean, but in retrospect she realized he was a carrier of the trust of the Quran. He was strict about the Quran, not angry with her. Today she understands, but at the time, this, too, was a struggle.

Not only was Charlotte the only woman in her community memorizing the Quran, but she also faced extra challenges as a black woman. "I'm still challenged a lot of times, because people see this black woman and they're like, 'No.' I end up having to recite, and then the people who know Quran will say, 'Oh, okay.'"

Charlotte struggled with community members who were jealous and mean-spirited. She knew in her heart that learning the Quran was a great and blessed endeavor, but men and women in her community were less than supportive. "Some people would even go so far as to say, 'Oh you think you're so much because you know the Quran.'" But this type of criticism did not find its way into Charlotte's heart. She was able to separate herself from their comments and retain the loftiness of her goal. "No. No. You know what I mean? There's no way you can think you're so much. There's no way you can be arrogant and the Lord allows you to learn this Quran! Those two don't go together. Those are two foreign things."

Still, Charlotte did sometimes feel hurt or disappointed. Facing the incessant talk was not easy, and even her (now ex) husband was hostile about her memorization. But she found solace in the Quran itself. Their criticism pushed her deeper into her journey, and the Quran would comfort her, "I had a lot of hurt, but every time I would be hurt or disappointed or feeling bad or sad, I could always turn to Quran. I'd cry, but the Quran would always make it okay. I could get in the Quran and forget all my problems, and forget all the bad talk, forget all the sadness. I could get lost in it..."

Memorizing the Quran changed her deeply. "It made me more humble. It made me more forgiving. It made me more tolerant. It made me kinder. It made me more patient. It made me more loving. It completely changed me from what I was before. It's like 180 degrees because, mind you, I was twenty-eight years old when I accepted Islam. I had lived a lifetime before then."

Fortunately, things are different for Charlotte now. She oversees religious affairs at the largest mosque in her city. "It's a gigantic, beautiful masjid, and an international community. The imams and administration, everybody respects me. They ask me for my advice on things." She is included in decision making and is a main teacher. Only rarely now do people question her ability or her accomplishments. "It's just new people who don't know me. I'll get that, like, 'What's she doing? Who is this black lady?'"

She remains passionate about the Quran, Islam, and learning in general. She is greatly concerned about the Muslim family and the younger generations. Her years of learning were always peppered with teaching the youth, and now she is devoted and concerned. She worries about the influence of electronic devices, the overwhelming influence of the public school, and the 'busy' that every family seems to suffer from. She sees cure in the Quran, but not enough of our young people devoted to learning it. She was adamant that women must learn the Quran. It is up to us women to set the standard and preserve the tradition. She grew serious and thoughtful during our interview and said, "Just be an inspiration to the ladies, because we're going to die, too, and we're going to stand before Allah ﷻ. I've heard ladies say, 'Well, I don't have to pray because my husband's praying,' but, no. Your husband is not going to be able to carry any of your burdens. What about your children? We're losing our children to this *dunyā*. We have to be very careful to make sure that we give them something that's for real, and the only thing that's real is that Quran. That's what Allah ﷻ left us, the Quran and the sunna of the Prophet, peace be upon him! That's what we need to hold tight, especially nowadays, because it seems like Yawm al-Qiyāma (the Day of Judgement) is upon us, when you look at the world."

Method

Charlotte's method was to commit to memory about two pages every night. She memorized both the Arabic and the English translation. She studied books of *tafsīr* to try to better understand what the verses were saying. As her skills in Arabic improved, she began to see miracles in the Arabic language as well. "It's just mind-blowing to me, how small the English is and how big the Quranic Arabic is. It is just a love affair that's been going on almost forty years, and it's still that way. It hasn't changed. You never stop learning."

But Arabic was not her native tongue, so she committed to

memorizing the English along with the Arabic. It would take her most of the night, but she remembered this time with great love and wistfulness, "Like I said, it was such a magical time. I don't remember eating. I don't remember sleeping. It was such a—maybe magical is not the word—but that's as big as English goes."

Her nighttime memorization was not just a straightforward learn and recite. She struggled to correct her mistakes, to remember work from the previous evening, and to raise her own standard of work. "It was just like knitting. I would knit together what I had learned before and, if anything wasn't up to his standards, then I would have to clean that up and do it again and also do the next two pages. A lot of times I would do more than two pages, just because I had such a hard time and I wanted to be the best one in his class. And *al-ḥamdu lillāh*, I was."

Now that she is a *ḥāfiẓa*, she reviews regularly. She reads, listens, and recites Quran during her prayer. It is a continuous learning process, and review has become part of her life.

Pointers

1. Memorize daily.
2. Memorize at night.
3. Memorize the Arabic and the English translation.
4. Study and read *tafsīr* books.
5. Use competition to help and encourage yourself.
6. Continuously review.

Advice

Charlotte calls on women and girls who begin the journey of memorization to, "Keep trying, even if you have to keep it a secret." She suggests constant listening, even when doing other activities. "I used to just keep my earplugs in, and I guess people thought I was listening to music." But she was listening to the Quran. This constant listening was certainly one of the reasons she succeeded, but perhaps her dogged determination was her best friend on this road.

She advises all of us, "Try your best, because Allah says He makes it easy. The next thing you know, you'll have it. Keep trying to get that knowledge, because it's a wonderful thing. It makes all the difference. It takes care of everything. Don't let anybody stop you and don't get discouraged. Put all your trust and hope in Allah. Even if you don't memorize it all, which is very intensive, memorize some of the suras. We always have to learn, that's part of Islam. Just keep trying. That's all I got to say about that. That's what worked for me."

Tips

1. Don't give up.
2. Listen constantly.
3. Don't quit memorizing because the 'whole' seems too much. Memorize only a little, that's OK, but don't give up completely.

2. Raneem

Raneem's journey started when she was very young. Like many, her learning was informal in the beginning. She attended Islamic school and Saturday school and participated in whatever Quran curriculum they offered and, as a Syrian-American, spent her summers in Syria attending summer Quran circles. Raneem was a talented and motivated learner, even as a child. As she went from one learning space to another, she learned whatever part of the Quran was being taught that season. As a result, she skipped some parts of the Quran and memorized others more than once. But by the time she was twelve years old, she had filled in the gaps and was a *ḥāfiẓa*. She had not memorized the Quran from the beginning to the end, but rather sporadically and in bursts. She said about this unusual beginning, "It gave me an idea, a feel for what I was getting myself into. And gave me a feel for the *muṣḥaf* itself, the Meccan suras, the Madinan suras, the different themes, where things are, things like that."

As Raneem grew older, she continued to learn and study the Quran. She was a young *tajwīd* expert at school and, as a late teen, made a life-changing decision. During her trips back and forth from Syria, Raneem had heard of both types of *ijāza*: the *tajwīd* certificate, and the memorization certificate. It was rare for anyone not living in Syria to seek the memorization certificate. The commitment and devotion necessary were just not practical for most. But Raneem, in consultation with her family and *tajwīd* instructor, decided to try for it. Though she had worked with her *tajwīd* instructor for a couple of years already, she credited this decision as the beginning of a completely different relationship, one that was not all butterflies and roses. Raneem reflected, "I think I was destined to have Anse Maha as a teacher. Everyone gets their match, and she was mine. She knew how to push my buttons. She made me competitive with myself. After every recitation, she would say something like, 'Oh, is that it?' and very rarely would she ever say anything nice." While some people may have felt frustrated by the lack of encouragement, Raneem just kept pushing. The summer I met her, she was memorizing and reciting more than thirty pages a day to her teacher. In my mind, I imagined it like Han Solo putting the Millenium Falcon into hyperspace and disappearing into the galaxy. She was so focused; she could shut out the noises and little conversations of every one of the thirty girls in the Quran camp.

"Sometimes she'd even make fun of me. I remember making a mistake where I changed the *ḥarakāt* (short vowel sounds), and it changed the meaning of the word, and she stopped me and repeated it, and she was like, 'Really, Raneem? Really?' She just started laughing, but it was all good-natured."

The role of the teacher is often pivotal, speeding up or slowing down progress. Students of Quran can memorize on their own, but to check on learning and grow in expertise, they need to be working with a Quran teacher. Raneem was a star student with a difficult-to-impress instructor. This strict attitude was cushioned in sincere devotion. Though Raneem spoke about Anse Maha's unsympathetic responses to her progress, she also recognized her sacrifice.

"She made it very easy for me. A lot of times she would take a taxi to *my* home. She really bent over backwards for me."

Raneem did work with other *tajwīd* teachers. She remembered the time she had an appointment to review the first five *ajzā'* as one solid block. She was so nervous. "And then she chose a page from the sixth *juzu'*. I had come in prepared for the first five, so my jaw just dropped. I was kind of freaking out, you know? She looked at me, and said, 'Just kidding. Now you won't be afraid when I ask you from the first five.'" So she did have some comic relief.

For memorizers working toward a final *ijāza* or certification of their work while living in Syria, the dreaded final recitation was nerve-racking. Sheikh Kurdi was over ninety years old and still testing and accepting or refusing students as carriers of his *ijāza*. For the successful, that day is the crowning day. For some, it means closure. And for some, it means an opening. But whatever it means, people tend to remember that day down to the smallest detail.

Raneem spent most of the night before her test reviewing and praying *salat al-ḥāja* (the prayer of need). She was already nervous, and she became downright scared when the woman right before her did not pass. She walked out devastated. She said, "Then it was my turn. His grandkids kept opening the drapes and stuff, and at that point I was just really scared. They introduced me and, at that point, I zoned out; I don't even know what they were saying." Her test began, and he asked her to recite from a number of different places, asked her about the rules of *tajwīd*, and had her recite from the *Jazariyya*, which is a long poem about the rules of *tajwīd* that is part of the required learning for the *ijāza*. The final sura he asked her to recite was Surat al-Fatḥ, which Raneem found significant and hoped that the final part of the test would indicate the beginning of the next stage of her journey. Fatḥ means opening, and she hoped for ease and success as a *ḥāfiẓa*.

She completed her recitation and sat quietly, unsure of how she had done. "Anse Maha came and gave me a thumbs up. She didn't even tell me. She just smiled and gave me a thumbs up. I didn't know if she meant I was done or I had passed. I just remember bursting into tears. I didn't know what it meant, but I just felt so happy that I was done. I cried the whole way back, and I can't even explain why. It was just an overwhelming experience." Raneem became the first

Syrian-American to receive her *ijāza* for the memorization of the Quran (rather than the *ijāza* for *tajwīd* alone), and she continues to teach and recite to this day.

Method

Raneem used a *muṣḥaf* that was broken into six parts. Each binding contained five *ajzā'* of the Quran, and the print was fairly large. She used this *muṣḥaf* to memorize.

Her Islamic high school teachers recognized her skill at *tajwīd* and asked her to teach the other students once a week. Because of that, they offered her that hour on the other school days to work on her own memorization. "I took advantage of the hour. I would be in a room by myself, and every single day I would memorize a page. I had charts and graphs, because I had to prove I wasn't just sitting there for an hour doing nothing. At the end of the quarter I would have to show my work, and I would just lay it out like, 'Here it is. I started here and I ended here.'" At night she would review the page she had learned that day in school along with the one she had learned the day before. She would continue adding pages until she reached twenty or the end of the sura. She would take those pages she had worked on all year with her on her summer break to Syria and recite them to her *tajwīd* instructor.

She knew colloquial Arabic. They spoke it at home and she visited Syria often. But, having never studied in Arabic schools, she felt that her language skills were not much help. So she created a system to help herself understand what she was memorizing. She would annotate her *muṣḥaf*. With a pencil, she would put a letter above the word or words in question and then list their meanings in the margin. "At first, I was just defining the words. I know there are *maṣāḥif* that already do that, but I did it anyways, and it was sort of a learning experience. And then the more I went through, and you can see this in my *maṣāḥif*, the more I progressed, the more the annotations would get longer and deeper. Not just definitions, but more like the feel."

Pointers

1. Find time to memorize and then use it.
2. Keep track of progress.
3. Use the day to memorize and the night to review.
4. Look up meanings and work to understand.
5. Do review of large sections seasonally.

Advice

Raneem's advice to girls or women who want to memorize the Quran is simple. "They have to be self-motivated. They can't be doing it for anyone else or for any type of status or anything like that. You must have love and passion and perseverance. It's not easy, and it's a lifelong journey. It's not like, 'Well, I'm going to embark on it now, and then I'll be done in a few years and that's it.'"

She continued, "They shouldn't be focusing on the memorization aspect as much as the meanings of the verses, and what they felt at certain times reciting them. With time, different verses will mean different things. It's not a sport or a hobby or anything like that. It's a serious matter, and you're responsible. The more you know, the more you're responsible for."

Raneem advises new memorizers to face any opposition with incredulity. Her experience was always that the women in her family knew the Quran better than the men, so the idea that anyone might oppose her because she was a woman was both new and shocking. Her response to the idea that people should avoid memorizing for fear of forgetting was memorable, "That's a reverse way of looking at things. You could extend that to so much. You could be like, 'Ignorance is bliss. I don't want to learn anything about the *deen*, because, if I do, then it's going to be held against me' Or, 'I don't want to get too close to God, because, if I do, then I'm going to be tried and tested.' It's false logic.

"I think the whole point of that hadith is to emphasize that it's lifelong. That once you memorize something, don't let it go. You're never completely finished. That's what I get from it. I don't get, 'Don't memorize in the first place.'"

She also made an important point regarding expectations. Raneem reminds us all that memorizing Quran is a dynamic process and a lifelong journey, that we will all still see hard times and even struggle with faith. Memorizing the Quran is not a cure for being human. But she says, "When I go through different phases in life, I know where to turn in the Quran. For example, if I'm struggling with my faith, I turn to the Meccan suras, because they're about faith. And it helps me. When I'm going through an easier time, I might read the Madinan suras. I have a sense of where to turn in the Quran." Memorizing makes us familiar enough with the Quran that it remains accessible to us, even in darker times. Raneem also advises all learners to stay open to understandings. She said that the very process of repetition means that it will become ingrained, and its meaning may appear later in life—just at a needed moment.

Tips

1. Don't compete with others, compete with yourself to get better each day.
2. Know the meaning of what you are learning. Read through a *tafsīr* book or translation. Use a dictionary.
3. Spend time listening to Quran.
4. Appreciate the time your teacher is donating to you and respect that by staying focused.
5. Use the learning methods that work for you in other subjects. Use charts and graphs if they help you. Study in quiet if that helps. Be aware of what works for you.
6. Make notes in your *muṣḥaf*. They can be *tajwīd* reminders, important insights, or anything that occurs to you. This will all help the memorization process.

3. Madiha

Meet Madiha, a young woman of Indian-Pakistani origin. Born and raised in the US, she's currently in her thirties and memorized the Quran between the ages of eighteen and twenty-one while in Damascus, Syria. She went to an Islamic school when she was young and had memorized the 29th and 30th *ajzā'* before she set off for Syria. She decided to embark on the journey after graduating from high school, when she went through a low point in her life and found herself continuously making the *du'ā'*, "Oh Allah, I want to memorize the Quran." Madiha spent her first year in Damascus getting her *ijāza* in *tajwīd*, and then she went straight into memorizing.

In the beginning, she found it difficult, as did most of the women I interviewed. In those early days, it took her an hour to memorize a page. She used to read an *āya* once, and then a second time, and then connect them, and so on.

Madiha felt that memorizing was especially hard from the beginning (Surat al-Baqara) until she completed Surat al-Tawba. She spoke about the process of repenting while memorizing. As she memorized, she would continue to turn to Allah ﷻ in repentance, humility, and thankfulness. Her continuous *tawba* was one thing that made it easier to memorize.

Madiha gained wisdom and maturity while memorizing, and now continues to grow in them after having accomplished the feat and having time to reflect on it. When asked what pitfalls she encountered during her memorization, she answered, "I feel like the answer to that question is so different for everybody. That's what makes it so amazing, because we end up really having a relationship with the Quran. I remember sometimes there'd be *āyāt* that I would have such a hard time memorizing, and then when I looked back at the meaning, I saw that they pointed to something within me that I had to change or fix. I was blessed, too, because I had teachers around me to help with that. I wasn't just memorizing—the words weren't just coming off my tongue—but I was really feeling what was going on."

Having teachers and mentors who were in tune with the spiritual aspect of memorization helped Madiha on her journey. She was able to connect the dots between the effort it takes to memorize and the internal struggle to become a person worthy of carrying the Quran. There were moments of great serendipity; Madiha recalled the numerous times she would be memorizing certain verses and, everywhere she went, they would be mentioned. Sometimes in classes, other times in more casual lectures, or in subject studies. She began to see the Quran as integrally connected to her life, and this helped her both remember the verses and implement them.

The journey to memorize has many travelers, and Madiha both appreciated and struggled with the young women who were walking with her on the path. The younger girls—some in their early teens—would often make her feel like she was late to the game. She regretted not starting earlier and saw the ease with which they memorized the verses. On the other hand, she enjoyed the companionship of those who were nearer to her age, and together they recognized the benefit of beginning this journey fully from their own decision and motivation. The younger girls had parents encouraging and pressuring them. Madiha had her own internal drive and desire to be a *ḥāfiẓa*. The choice to leave the United States and travel in order to memorize meant that she was distanced from distractions. It was sometimes lonely work, and there were certainly difficulties in the choice, but, for Madiha, being away from school, work, and household responsibilities was a key to her success.

Madiha did not announce her new status as '*ḥāfiẓa*', and in fact, almost ten years later, few people know that she is indeed a walking Quran. "It wasn't like I was going around with this title on, you know what I mean?" Once, though, when she started laughing in a conversation, someone who did know about her accomplishment said, "Oh, it's so nice to see that you still laugh." The comment was uncomfortable for Madiha. She said, "Sometimes people think that, if you become religious or you're pursuing your religious studies, that you all-of-a-sudden become like this super-strict person. I think having those teachers around in Syria showed me the opposite. Becoming more connected just means you're living life to its fullest, in the right way."

Madiha has heard some imams say that women should not

memorize the Quran because they get their periods and do not recite on those days, but since most of these comments came after she had memorized, they did not affect her journey. She said that she never thought about 'could she or couldn't she'—she wanted to memorize Quran, and it never occurred to her that anyone might discourage her. She does think about the great responsibility that rides on her shoulders now that she is a *ḥāfiẓa*—the responsibility to hold on to the Quran, to carry it with her, and to live it. But this is a beautiful responsibility, and she encourages women to do it because it was such a life-changing thing for her. "I would definitely want someone else to be able to experience that."

Method

Madiha's method of memorizing was pretty straightforward. She would learn each verse separately and then connect them together. In order to learn each verse, she would listen to an audio recording and recite along with the reciter. In this way, she could check her pronunciation and timing. As she recited, she would note if the sheikh reciting would start the next word before or after her, and then adjust her *mudūd* (elongations) accordingly. It also helped to have the recitation ingrained in her mind as she worked to remember and recite the verses in her prayer. Arabic was also key. The Arabic language can feel overwhelming, but it helped Madiha memorize the Quran. Memorizing the vocabulary can feel new and daunting, but, for Madiha, it was learning grammar that opened doors for her. It helped her remember the diacritical marks and train her tongue correctly. When she was in doubt, Arabic grammar helped her know what came next in the verse.

Pointers

1. Learn Arabic as you go along; grammar is especially helpful.
2. Read what you are memorizing in your salat.
3. Listen to an audio recording and recite aloud with the reciter.

Advice

Madiha advises women everywhere to memorize Quran. The experience is worth the effort and time that goes into it. Her advice for success on the road of memorizing is to stay in *tawba.*

Tawba is the state of being in repentance. For Madiha, it was not about repenting once and moving on, but a process of growth that knitted her heart to the Quran, and her life to her religion. The Prophet ﷺ used to seek forgiveness seventy times a day according to many narrations, and, for Madiha, continuous repentance was key to her accomplishment.

Her experience was unique because she was able to travel and set aside her responsibilities for the sake of memorizing the Quran, and she recognizes that not everyone can do that, but still encourages thinking about taking time out. As writers will go to short writing workshops in order to get a quick start on a novel, memorizers could set aside a weekend or a week to get deeply into memorizing, or maybe an entire month in the summer, in order to start the process. Once you have started, it will be hard to let it go.

Finally, Madiha encourages women to find other women walking the same path. Having companionship is both encouraging and motivating. Seeing other women memorizing underlines the possibility in your own journey and, for some, ignites their competitive spirit and sets a fire under their feet to continue. As long as the intention remains clean and clear, a little competition can be healthy and help you to get over the humps and little difficulties.

Tips

1. Be around people who have already memorized the Quran.
2. Be in circles where you can review with each other.
3. Don't insist that you or your children finish within a certain amount of time, because it is something that is a part of your every day, forever. If you put a time limit of say, three years, it's so much easier to just stop it altogether after those three years.

4. Aziza

Aziza is of Indo-Pakistani origin, a mother of four, and active in her community in the Midwest. She states that, although it had been a dream of hers to memorize the Quran from the age of twenty-four, she was thirty-eight before she made a firm commitment to do so. Until then, she had kind of started on and off. "After I had one child it was kind of doable, but the more children I had, the further behind I always seemed. But I never let go of that dream."

At the age of thirty-eight, Aziza found herself at the pinnacle of her career. She had gone from teacher to administrator to principal, and then to district administrator for a public school system. As that job came to an end, she stood at a crossroads. She had to decide if she wanted to start looking for another job or take a break from her career and memorize Quran—or if she should try to do both. She personally hadn't found success trying to memorize 'on the side' while she worked and took care of her family, and one of her mentors encouraged her to take some time off and concentrate on memorizing. Aziza considered other factors, including her family, and decided to take the time to memorize. "It was really kind of time for me to stay home with my children and regroup back at the home front... I'm so glad I did, because from thirty-eight to forty-two I just dedicated all my time to taking care of my family and memorizing. I finished at forty-two."

When asked if she was discouraged to memorize the Quran because she's a woman or other things that naysayers point to, she replied, "None of that ever really made sense to me, because obviously memorizing the Quran is such a blessed thing. Any interaction that you have with the Quran, it's just so cleansing and purifying and such a breath of fresh air that I can't imagine something so good could be bad for you. No, it's not a good thing to leave the Quran after you've interacted with it for a long time, but who says that's going to happen? Why would we use that as a reason not to interact with the Quran at all? That's just silly."

Aziza feels that in memorizing the Quran she gained a skill that will be with her forever, "Now that I have this skill of reading and memorizing Quran, it's like riding a bike. Whenever you come back to it, you just bring that skill out." Now that Aziza is back at work and still caring for her family and her other community responsibilities, she has less time to devote to maintaining what she learned, but this does not concern her. "You won't put in eight hours a day like you did before, but you will put in whatever you can. You will revise whenever you can." Aziza misses the days of Quran and says, "Maybe there will be another time in my life when I will be able to put in another couple of years, just dedicated solely to the Quran."

Although there were obstacles and difficult times along the journey, Aziza felt that Allah ﷻ opened the door for her to be able to do this. Raising four kids and having household chores to do without any extended family close by, she was worried that, even without work, she would not be able to manage. But help always arrived in some form or other.

One time, a woman knocked on her door and said, "I'm looking for a job." She hired her to help out around the house with laundry, cooking, and other household chores. When this housekeeper quit, she thought, "Oh, that's it. I'm not going to memorize anymore. I tried; it's over now." Then someone else would come along. It was like that throughout her whole process. And within one week of completing her memorization, the housekeeper she employed at the time quit. She never found anyone to replace her because she'd reached her Quranic goal and had less need for household help.

Aziza joined a local class of young learners and memorized with them. Her memorization happened in a Midwestern city, in a typical memorizing class—but she was indeed an anomaly because she was almost forty years old! About her peers, Aziza says, "We all sat on the floor. There were four-year-olds and six-year-olds and seven-year-olds and ten-year-olds. I think the oldest were like thirteen and fourteen. They were like my teachers, my mentors. That was the other irony! I was coming from a position as an administrator at the district level, where I was giving orders, and now I was taking orders from four-year-olds. They were correcting me, telling me where I went wrong; they were almost making fun of me. I mean, in a cute sort of way. If I were them, I would have made fun of someone like me. Like, what's this old lady doing here?"

Aziza had some touching interactions with her fellow students, "I remember one of the girls—I think she was in eighth grade. I ran into her later, after I finished, and she was like, 'I heard you finished! *Subḥān Allah*, if you can do it, anyone can do it.' I was taken aback and thought, 'Wait a minute, what does that mean?' She probably thought there was no hope for me."

Before launching her Quran memorization project, Aziza had been a busy community member, running classes for young Muslims herself while teaching and supporting other women. Once she started memorizing, she was less visible. She just did not have time. Her head and heart were filled with the Quran. She knew it was temporary and that memorizing the Quran would give her a stronger foundation with which to reach out in her *daʿwa* work (calling to Islam), but, still, people's comments sometimes gave her pause. "People were confused. 'What are you doing? Memorizing is just for little kids, and you are an adult. You are a speaker, so you should be out there giving speeches.' So I'd get that slack, and then I'd see these little kids running circles around me—you know, passing me up. But then I just kept saying, 'No. I can't imagine that this would be a bad thing for me. It's about purification and effort, and that's all I'm going for.'"

At the completion of her memorization project, Aziza held an elaborate party for herself. She was, in a way, coming out to the community again. She wanted to demonstrate to the women and girls that they could indeed memorize the entire Quran. She wanted the young girls to imagine themselves in a big celebratory party. She said that young girls often dream of their wedding, and, while she did not want to stop that dream, she wanted to add a dream to their imaginations, the dream of wearing a glittery dress and crown and standing before friends and family having completed the memorization of the Quran. The moms were also part of her motivation to hold a party. She recognized that women in their thirties often decide that it is over for them, and they devote all their time to their children, neglecting their own growth. But she wanted to encourage them to change that thinking and hold on to their own dream of memorizing the Quran. The party was her way of calling out to girls and women and giving them a concrete example of a dream realized.

Method

Aziza found a method that worked for her, and so she adhered to it throughout her memorization. "My brain was not functioning at an elementary child's level in the sense that kids can just absorb information and facts, and their recall ability is a lot sharper than ours. Our brains can think in different ways, more analytical, but we just don't have that [memorization] ability. Given that, I had to adjust. I think I had to work about ten times harder than my fellow students, who were third and fourth graders."

Her method was very specific. She would read, review, increase the amount, work on the text looking for patterns, sleep, and then come back to it. She said, "First, I'd just read it. I'd have to read it like fifty times. I started out with three lines, and then it became ten lines, and then it became one page. Then towards the end, it was becoming two pages, but I could never do more than two pages, whereas I saw some kids who were able to do even multiple pages at a time." Aziza recognized that as an adult she did not have the same memorizing skill as the children, but she had other skills: determination and analytical capabilities. She would read and repeat and read and repeat and read and repeat so many times that a child would certainly tire and rebel, but Aziza would get better each time. Then she would use her analytical skills to knit the verses into her mind.

"I'd read it another ten, fifteen times, and this time I would look for patterns. I would look for words that I knew. I'd read the context of the story, I'd look for patterns in the page and I started kind of putting those patterns together. Then I would sleep on it. The next morning, I would start to solidify it." Aziza used her understanding of learning to help herself. She recognized her strengths and weaknesses and used her strengths and intelligences to help her accomplish her goal.

She broke up her learning of each section into four steps, "I always needed to sleep between step two and step three, because that's how it would somehow gel in my mind. I had to keep up with the rhythm. I had to keep up with this schedule because if I broke away from it, I would lose momentum and fall behind."

Pointers

1. Read and repeat and repeat and repeat and repeat and repeat...
2. Look for patterns in the language, the story, the *tajwīd*, and understand context. In between steps two and three, sleep on it.
3. Read multiple times.
4. Recite.

Advice

As a teacher and community leader, Aziza has thought a lot about memorizing the Quran and how to advise others interested in the journey.

"There are few things that are going to keep us grounded and really save us in the end, and Quran is one of them. If you make Quran your friend and build a relationship with it, that's your insurance. That's your protection in life. I think people can understand this concept because they're seeing a lot of hard times. We're seeing people taking off their hijab, we're seeing people leave the faith, we're seeing people get into relationships that are harmful, we're seeing unsteady homes where there's a lot of fighting, a lot of arguments, no peace, no happiness. The Quran is a protection against all of that." She hopes that people will develop a healthy relationship with the Quran—interacting with it, reading it, working on it, even if they do not actually memorize the entire book.

She encourages people who are lonely to seek friendship in the Quran. "It's your friend and it's your place of peace." And for those with anxiety and concern, "It's your safe haven. It whisks you away from the worries and troubles of the world." Aziza's experience is that the Quran is a healing for anyone and everyone. "It just does wonders for you."

Aziza felt strongly that Muslims, and especially Muslim women, should return to serious study of the Quran. Engaging with the Quran is an important part of the process of building a relationship that results in true submission to Allah's will. "You always know that Allah is in control of your life, but being that close to the Quran helps you truly feel it, truly trust Him, and gain the closeness that enables you to ask for all your needs from Him."

Tips

1. Never give up. You will think that you cannot do it. You will hit road blocks, and you will think this is not for you, but never give up. Every day, try. Even if it is just a little bit, never leave it. There will be waves of ease and there will be blockades, too. Just hold on tight in those hard times and there will be times of lots of *baraka* (blessings) and openness. But don't give up.
2. Be consistent. Don't leave a day. Don't think, "Oh, one day is okay to miss." Because that's how you fall behind.
3. Oftentimes people don't want to give up their lifestyles. They don't want to give up going to the movies or hanging out with friends or even family. Just hanging out. People don't want to give that up. But if you're going to memorize Quran, you have to give a lot of that up. People will get together, they will do things, they will do fun things, and you might not be able to do that. You must give it up for a certain little bit of time if you want to immerse yourself enough to complete the entire Quran.

5. Serene

Serene grew up in a Midwestern community with a large population of Syrian-Americans and started memorizing Quran at around three years old. She feels her community facilitated it for her, so it was easy. She went to Sham for the first time when she was thirteen, and found that she enjoyed memorizing the Quran. She felt homesick during that trip, but she focused on Quran and ended up memorizing Surat al-Baqara in three weeks.

Looking back on that time, she recalls thinking, "Wow, this is something that I am actually good at." It wasn't anything like school. School was very stressful, but the Quran felt like it was calling her. During her school-age years, Serene memorized about five or six *ajzā'*.

When she returned to Sham at the age of fifteen, her teachers encouraged her to learn *tajwīd* before proceeding further with memorization. Although she was not that excited about *tajwīd*, she trusted her teachers' advice and started working on her *ijāza* in *tajwīd*.

On her pairing with her teacher, she fondly remembers, "They put me with a teacher, I think according to the type of temperament I have and the type of temperament the teacher had, because we were total opposites, and it worked for me. *Al-ḥamdu lillāh*."

She recited the Quran with *tajwīd* to her teacher for hours each day, and right before her sixteenth birthday she achieved an *ijāza* in *tajwīd*. Now she had the tools and the tongue to memorize without error, so she continued with her memorization.

As Serene became more serious about memorizing the Quran, she still didn't discuss it with anyone. "I didn't even talk to my parents about it because I felt that, since I struggled in school in certain subject areas, this would be something else I would struggle with, and I didn't want to be a failure at it because it's something I loved so much, so I kept it to myself.

"I didn't want to be that person talking about how they're memorizing Quran, and I didn't want to be known as the goody-two-shoes. I remember thinking, 'Oh, it's not really the cool thing to do. None of my other friends are memorizing.' And I didn't really have anybody to share it with. I felt like it was just literally me and Allah and that's it. It was the closest I ever felt to Him. It was amazing."

Upon returning to the States, she set up a schedule for herself. She started with Surat Āl 'Imrān, which was easy for her, but she struggled with al-A'rāf. She was tested by different women in her community. Between Saturday school and her regular Islamic school, she was memorizing different portions of the Quran at the same time. Looking back, she speaks in awe of that time in her life. "We had no social media, I had no laptop; I had no cellphone. Literally all I did was sit on my bed and memorize Quran."

When asked what her parents thought of what she was doing, she smiles, "Of course they liked it. They were happy, and I loved it. I felt very good about it." Through all of this, she remembers how she got reminders every so often from her teacher in Syria not to become arrogant about what she was doing and to keep her intentions pure. "'You know, memorizing isn't anything if you're not going to live by it.' She would just drill that into my head."

Though Serene began memorizing the Quran because of its fluidity and ease, during her journey, there were many times that she struggled. She reflected, "I've never shared these stories with anybody. But I would cry to Allah all the time. On a day-to-day basis, alone in my room. Like hours. And my parents had no clue. I felt like that strengthened my relationship with Allah; making *du'ā'* and asking Him to help me through, because it's something I really, really wanted." Serene realized that the Quran is unlike any other subject. She laughed and said that we can't get CliffsNotes® for the Quran. The Quran is God's words and needs human work and intention. Even the teacher is irrelevant if the memorizer is not willing to put in the work. She said, "You can't even say, 'Oh, let me try this teacher and that teacher; maybe that will help me memorize...' No. It's not about that. It's about having a pure heart."

Serene saw her memorization as a letter she was writing to Allah ﷻ. As a young woman, she went through a period in her life that she felt she needed to make amends for. So her memorization became a very private and personal conversation between her and Allah ﷻ. She said, "I felt like I almost wanted to make amends by memorizing the Quran and by getting closer to Allah through it. I decided to dedicate my life to it because of something specific. You know what I mean? It was more like when you apologize to somebody, you write them letters. For me, memorizing the Quran was my letter to Allah. That was my way to make amends."

For Serene, the whole process was dynamic. "Throughout it, I would read certain verses as if I was reading them for the first time. I know other people say that, too. It's amazing, because it would touch me at the time that I needed it the most." Her feeling of amazement and wonderment at the Quran continues. She will still pick up the Quran and have a moment of clarity and say to herself, "I can't believe

I didn't realize that this is what it meant."

At the age of nineteen, Serene decided that she wanted to complete the entire Quran and recite it from memory to someone. She went back to Syria, but with only five months to achieve her goal. She didn't have the option to extend her trip. She understood the enormity of this trip, and described how she prepared herself for it, "I remember saying to myself that I wanted to memorize it before my twentieth birthday. Before I went, though, I had to do a pre-cleansing, like a preparation for it. I'm a firm, strong believer in doing that when it comes to anything Quran or *sīra* or hadith related—just purify your heart and your intention and your mind and just really, clearly understand why it's being done and for whom, which is only Allah."

This is where Serene's journey reached another level. She described the progression of her recitation with her teacher: "In the beginning, I hid behind a pillow, and I remember how scared I was. My voice was crackling and I was nervous. It got easier, but my teacher never complimented me or gave me any positive reinforcement. Never. I remember one day in the first week or second week, she took the pillow and threw it. That was it. She wouldn't let me hide behind that pillow anymore. And I feel like I kicked off from there. It just totally changed things, built my confidence.

"I did all of Surat al-Tawba in one day. I remember her being shocked because al-Tawba is fourteen pages. She looked at me in a shocked way and then kind of smiling at the same time. That, to me, was all the positive reinforcement I needed. *Al-ḥamdu lillāh*, I took off from there and started knocking off maybe ten to twenty pages from then on for the next month. After that, I started doing twenty to thirty pages, and then I just kept increasing."

Serene describes the grueling schedule she kept herself on, "I would literally memorize all day, every single day, and I wouldn't let anybody talk to me. I would sit in a corner facing the wall. I was determined. I'd never been that determined in my life, and I still haven't found that determination in anything else.

"It was amazing, though, because at that time, I was sharing the experience with a really good friend of mine who was working on her *ijāza ʿal-ghaib*. She and I would stay in the kitchen until, honestly, two in the morning. We would only get one and a half to two hours of sleep every single night." Serene and her friend would test each other, sometimes breaking down and crying and other times cracking up in laughter. It was a personal journey that they shared with one another.

Serene's teacher had high standards for her students, and for Serene, she had certain requirements. "She would never test me unless I recited all of what I was memorizing in my *nawāfil* (supererogatory prayers). I would literally knock out maybe fifty *nawāfil* a day beside my regular sunna prayers. It was very, very hard for me to do that, because I'm not the most patient person in the world. It was so hard for me to have to do that. But she forced me. She would come to me and be like, 'Did you recite in your prayer?' There was one time I said no, and she actually left. She wouldn't test me. That's when I knew she was not joking. From then on, I never missed a day."

"In the end, I was able to memorize forty pages in one day, which is two *ajzā'*. When she first tested me on one *juzu'*, all she did was crack a smile." Once, when Serene was memorizing twenty pages a day, another mentor said to her, "One *juzu'*? Make them two." And Serene whispered to herself, "Challenge accepted." From that day on, she was able to complete two *ajzā'* per day, or forty pages. She had arrived in Syria with little over half of the Quran completed, and in the span of five months, she completed the twelve parts remaining. She became a *ḥāfiẓa*.

Today, Serene is teaching elementary-aged children the Quran. Some want to pursue full memorization, and she is cautiously encouraging. She applauds their intention to crown their parents, but encourages them to purify their intention and be ready to live the lifestyle of memorizing. She continues to review the Quran, working on holding on to her memorization. It took her one year and a half to review the forty-nine pages of Surat al-Baqara. She does not refer to herself as a *ḥāfiẓa*, and said, "If anybody ever called me that, I would be looking around like, 'Who are you talking about?' Because for me personally, I absolutely don't feel that way."

She spoke about her serious teacher's first comment at the conclusion of her memorization, "She pulled the Quran out of her bag and said, 'This is only the beginning.'" At first, it devastated Serene, she was hoping for closure, but, later, she realized that, as an American, her habit was to think of things in projects, with beginnings and ends, but now she was a *ḥāfiẓa* and the Quran had no end in her life.

Serene's journey started before she got married and continued after marriage and children. She struggled with young children, with following a husband from city to city, and with a stay-at-home-mom lifestyle. "After my first kid, it totally changed. It was literally an overnight thing. I was like 'Oh, my God. How do I incorporate Quran into this whole staying up at night thing with a child or waking up and all that?' I struggled. I don't think I did anything in the first two or three years of my first child's life."

Even though she saw a drastic change in her own ability to keep up with her Quran schedule, Serene did not agree with anyone who might discourage a woman from memorizing because of marriage or children. "I think that's bologna and it's very discouraging. I would never say that to a person."

She talked about her own experience as part of a lifelong learning process. "It's just like having a relationship. Except that this is the most important relationship in anybody's life, because it's your connection with Allah. Yeah, that's where I screwed up big time. Those three years. It's almost like you break up. But I think that I had to go through that in order to pick myself back up. Because you don't realize what you have until it's gone. That's how the *dunyā* works. Just like my teacher told me: 'If you don't show gratitude, it'll be taken away.' That's exactly what happened. Maybe I did get too cocky at one point in time."

Her years away from the Quran did not translate into anything but further conviction about the importance of memorizing Quran. Serene offered an interesting analogy. "It's kind of like the parent who has a teenager, and the teenager is just totally off the wall and rebellious. Would you say to that parent, 'Don't you wish you never had a kid?' No, you don't. Parents say *al-ḥamdu lillāh* for the experience and, you know, I've tried my best." And certainly Serene continues to try her best, reviewing and reciting the Quran continuously, seeking that elusive description of *ḥāfiẓa*.

Method

Serene's method was basic—reciting and repeating continuously and waiting for an unknown time when she could be tested. She reminisced, "I had a method. I just would recite, repeat, recite, repeat, recite, repeat. For everybody it's different; there are so many ways to memorize, and people just need to find their way." She never knew when her teacher would come to listen to her recite and test her. She said, "It's not that she wasn't good with time, she just had a billion other things to do, so she would come whenever she could. Sometimes she would show up at 2:00 pm, sometimes at 6:00 pm, sometimes at 8:00 pm, sometimes at 11:00 pm. Sometimes she wouldn't even show up." Having varied appointment times that were unknown encouraged Serene to work all day, every day, hoping to be ready whenever her teacher did arrive. Then she would start the whole cycle over again.

Pointers

1. Read.
2. Recite.
3. Repeat.
4. Rush to be ready and then sometimes...
5. Wait.
6. Repeat.

Advice

Serene encourages people of all ages to try to memorize the Quran and is emphatic about not putting an age limit on the endeavor. "I've witnessed people who are in their fifties and sixties who memorize it perfectly. I have a friend, her father is a physician, and for about five or six years he sat in his office and memorized Quran every day, and then he ended up getting his *ijāza* when he was in his sixties."

Serene emphasized self-reflection and self-improvement when memorizing. "It's like when a person puts their mind to it, and they ask Allah ﷻ to help, and they're sincere, and they have that good intention, then *in shā' Allāh* they'll have *tawfīq*. But really, those are the secrets to Quran. Sincerity, pure intentions, and a pure heart. Those are what allow a person to really dig deep and figure out, 'Okay, how am I treating people? How's my day-to-day with others? What am I talking about? What am I thinking about?' It's everything."

Serene further elaborated on the character building required for memorizing the Quran. She pointed out the disastrous effects of a judgmental attitude, or an attitude of arrogance. Either can slow down or completely stop the memorization process.

"I would say also have a non-judgmental attitude towards people of all kinds, regardless of whether they're covered in tattoos and piercings from head to toe, or they're covered in niqab from head to toe.

"The reason I say that is because a lot of people grow up, including myself, inside a community. We judge people based on the way they dress, and that's not fair. That affects your heart immediately. Like just thinking about other people in a negative way is almost a form of arrogance because you're considering yourself better than somebody else. I'd say to never, ever judge anybody. You don't know what's going on. They could be closer to Allah."

Serene also emphasized taking care of the relationships that are closest to us. She talked about parents and spouses and shared her own struggles with those relationships and how they affected her Quran. "I'd also advise people to have good relationships with others. It is important to make sure that our parents are very happy, no matter how difficult they can be, because they could be ten times worse. Our parents can be difficult, and still they're our parents. It doesn't matter. They can step on us, you know. Maybe I'm being extreme, but that's just how it is." Serene also advises the memorizer to be fair and kind to everyone she meets. "Just have good relationships with people, whatever situation you're in. I say that because the older I get, just day-to-day dealing with co-workers and people who might rub you the wrong way, I'm telling you firsthand, that will affect your Quran very easily. That's just something that I think about on a daily basis. Just fix little mishaps."

Serene advises us to keep a little note or sign near our beds, so that, when we retire for the night, we take the time to think about our day. To review the things we said and the things we didn't say. She advises us to go over everything and ask ourselves the hard questions of "Was that necessary to say?" "Do I need to be kinder?" This kind of self-reflection is difficult to do without the ego getting in the way. It is easy to fall into a reverie of how others wronged you. But Serene advises that we do it anyway, and think carefully. It will affect our ability to memorize Quran, and so it is important.

Tips

1. Focus on the inner self. A peaceful heart will memorize Quran better and faster.
2. Take care of your relationships. Especially with parents and spouse. These primary relationships affect the ability to memorize.
3. Do not be judgmental or cruel. Be kind and loving.

6. Hafsa

Hafsa was born and raised in Sudan. She moved to the States in 1979, when she was in her twenties. As a child, she memorized a few chapters of the Quran, and then in her early twenties, she learned the rules of *tajwīd*. When she moved to the United States, she found a new teacher to help her continue learning *tajwīd* and dabbled in memorizing at that time as well. She began to memorize Surat al-Baqara while she practiced her *tajwīd*, but she did not start memorizing seriously until she was sixty years old.

Hafsa drew inspiration from the example of one of her elders, and from a hadith of the Prophet ﷺ. Her elder was an illiterate woman who was seventy years old and decided to start learning. She learned the Arabic alphabet and went on to learn how to read. She then started memorizing the Quran and memorized it all. Age is not a factor in goodness. She referenced the beautiful words that Anas b.

Mālik reported the Prophet ﷺ as saying: "If the Resurrection were established upon one of you while he has in his hand a sapling, then let him plant it."[23]

عَنْ أَنَسِ بْنِ مَالِكٍ قَالَ: قَالَ رَسُولُ اللَّهِ صَلَّى اللَّهُ عَلَيْهِ وَسَلَّمَ: إِنْ قَامَتْ عَلَى أَحَدِكُمُ الْقِيَامَةُ وَفِي يَدِهِ فَسِيلَةٌ فَلْيَغْرِسْهَا

She did not feel that she was too old. She knew, of course, that she was older than most people who begin this journey, but with her mentor's example, and the words of the Prophet ﷺ in her heart, she stepped forth in faith.

Most of Hafsa's motivation came from a close understanding of the words of the Prophet ﷺ and the Quran itself. She mentioned the hadith in which Abdullah b. 'Amr reported: "The Prophet, peace and blessings be upon him, said, 'It will be said to the companion of the Quran: Recite and ascend as you recited in the world. Verily, your rank is determined by the last verse you recite.'"[24]

عَنْ عَبْدِ اللَّهِ بْنِ عَمْرٍو عَنْ النَّبِيِّ صَلَّى اللَّهُ عَلَيْهِ وَسَلَّمَ قَالَ: يُقَالُ لِصَاحِبِ الْقُرْآنِ اقْرَأْ وَارْتَقِ وَرَتِّلْ كَمَا كُنْتَ تُرَتِّلُ فِي الدُّنْيَا فَإِنَّ مَنْزِلَتَكَ عِنْدَ آخِرِ آيَةٍ تَقْرَأُ بِهَا

Hafsa emphasized how much she enjoyed reading Quran, and said that the times she spent with Quran were her best moments. It became her friend, her companion, and her treasure.

Her goal is to live the Quran. When she sees commands such as 'O Ye who Believe...

- {Bow down and prostrate yourselves and adore your Lord; and do good; that ye may prosper. . .}[25]
- {Seek help with patient perseverance and prayer. . .}[26]
- {Be conscious of your Lord; good is for those who do good in this world. . .}[27]

- {Avoid suspicion, for suspicion in some cases is a sin, and spy not on each other nor speak ill of each other behind their backs. . .}[28]

and the many other verses that begin with the call to believers to pay heed, she makes a special effort to practice what is commanded. She said about doing her best to adhere to all of Allah's injunctions in the Quran, "And if one deviates because of being human, you come back to it and you hear it echo anytime you want to do something that is not good."

Hafsa mentioned that some scholars say that people who memorize the Quran, 'hold the Quran.' And to her this means "that you have to do things accordingly—your eating, your drinking, your talking. You want to be one of the people who know the Quran and practice it. Increase your faith by practicing what you read." She equates the person who memorizes Quran and does not practice it with a donkey who is carrying a lot of books on his back. Memorizing and practicing are two sides of the same goal. The Quran is lived in our lives and recited with our tongues. Our hearts beat with its words, and our minds are made fresh and intelligent with its memorization. The blessing of the Quran is unending.

Method

Hafsa was working full-time as a high school teacher of Arabic and Quranic Studies in a local Islamic school when she began to memorize. Time was tight during her days, and she was no longer young. Recognizing the need for the seriousness and time-saving qualities of a qualified teacher, she looked far and wide within her city limits. Not finding what she was looking for, she was grateful to find a group that memorized through an online program. In addition, she found a local group of women who were working on their own, and began to meet with them to practice her recitation.

She started with the last five *ajzā'* of the Quran, and after she completed the 25th *juzu'*, she went back to al-Baqara and memorized from the first to the 25th. She didn't have a set amount that she memorized daily. It varied. Some days she did ten and a half pages, and some days less. Sometimes she recited six days out of the week, and other times only a few. All in all, it took her fifteen months and three weeks to complete her first *khitma*.

She memorized and recited after Fajr, and was sure to recite during her prayer. She reviewed often and taught what she knew. She was patient and steadfast. Day by day, she added verses and pages, until she had finally completed her memorization. She continues to review and teach the Quran.

Pointers

1. Get a qualified teacher.
2. Practice with a community of other memorizers.
3. Use the time after Fajr.
4. Recite during prayer.
5. Review and review and review.

Advice

Hafsa was adamant that anyone can memorize the Quran. No one is too busy or too old or too young or too anything. "You can make time for it. If you take time to do your Quran memorization and your studying of the Quran, it will bless your day and your time. You will have time for Quran. You will have time for other things that you never had time for! You just have to have the will and make time. Because people make time for other things, like some people make time for community service. Some people make time for going to the movies. If you do your memorization early in the morning, after Fajr prayer, that will be the best, and you will have no difficulties in doing it. You will become a better person. You will become a better mother. You will become a better teacher. You will become a better community leader."

She noted that many more men than women memorize the entire Quran, but she was clear in her advice to women about this trend. She said that when Allah ﷻ commands something, He does not command it only for men. "When Allah ﷻ says, 'Read and ascend,' He never said it is only for men." She added, "Although there are differences between men and women in some things, when it comes to worship and reading Quran and memorizing Quran and practicing Quran, it's one kind of worship." And everyone should do it.

Tips

1. Learn *tajwīd* first so you memorize correctly.
2. Memorize in the early morning after Fajr.
3. Don't take on too much at one time. See what you can handle and stick with it.
4. Review as you go along. "Quran doesn't like you to leave it and go. If you leave it, it will leave you."
5. Recite it in your prayer and it will stick.
6. Teach what you know. What you teach will stick in your mind.
7. It's never too late. You're never too old.

7. Nada

Nada started memorizing Quran when she was quite young, with teachers in her community and the help of her older sisters. She started seriously memorizing when she was twenty-four and moved to Syria, her parents' home-country, for three years.

Throughout her childhood, the Quran was what kept Nada stable. She saw the Quran as keeping her on track, and then when she graduated from college, it became a serious goal. "I was having a hard time finding a job. (Don't major in linguistics.) Nothing else was working, I was trying to apply to grad schools; I was trying a whole bunch of things. *Subḥān Allah*, a door to Sham opened, and I took that step."

She had been looking for 'something', and the Quran found her. It grounded her during a time of personal instability and gave her focus and a goal. Now she wanted the Quran, and she wanted her *ākhira*. Everything else just fell into place.

Nada grew up seeing examples of women who memorized the Quran, so she knew it could be done. But she still had some family members who discouraged her from memorizing. Some told her she did not need to memorize because she already had an *ijāza* in *tajwīd*. Others warned her of the responsibility, saying, "Be careful, because you have to commit to this for life. If you're not prepared for that, then I don't recommend you do this." She said it was inspiring to have cousins and other mentors who had memorized the Quran and were devoted to it, but the resistance from her family was difficult. Looking back, she recognizes the good intention in their warnings, and admits that some of that negativity helped strengthen her intention and resolve. She is grateful that it was not enough to stop her from setting out on the memorization journey.

"There's just another level of appreciation that you gain for the Quran through memorizing. It's something very special."

Nada's experience was marked with a closeness to Allah ﷻ and an ease in her endeavor, "During the whole process there was that sense of nearness to Allah ﷻ. You just always felt He was right there, He's got your back. There were just these little things, like you're going to *tasmīʿ* (recite what you've learned), and you're running late, and all the lights turn green, and it works out. Like the path was being paved for me as I was going. You think you're having a problem, but then *subḥān Allah*, things work out."

After memorizing, Nada returned to the USA and set herself to teaching. Ten years later, she realizes that most of her teaching has been very basic. Her students have been newcomers to Islam, those who need to learn to read, and those who are discovering the Quran for the first time in their lives. Some community members have scolded her for such basic teaching, insinuating that she need not waste her time on beginners. Since she has an *ijāza* in *tajwīd* and is a *ḥāfiẓa*, they felt she should be working on more serious students. But Nada believed that new learners need a lot of support, and she felt her role as teacher of anyone and everyone was valuable.

"Just being out there, I think, is important. Just being available to people who are interested. Because if people don't see others who have done it, they don't see it as possible."

Nada feels that one of the factors keeping women from memorizing the Quran, or even entering into a journey with the Quran, is the lack of female teachers to whom they can recite. "And *ḥifẓ* programs for women aren't very common. There are people who probably don't even know it's something you could do. It's never even crossed their mind."

Method

Nada had a very specific method when she first memorized the Quran, and she has a new method she uses now that she is reviewing and continuously working to memorize it better and better. Her first method was to read through the pages to be memorized first, to make sure her *tajwīd* was on point. That first reading would be done with an audio recording so that she could listen and match her own recitation. She would do the second reading on her own to make sure that she was comfortable with her own recitation and that it was fluent.

Her next step was to read and study the meaning. She said that understanding the meaning was key for her; she struggled to memorize anything that she did not understand. "*Subḥān Allah*, every time I did have struggles with an *āya*, it was because I wasn't understanding it properly, even grammatical things. For me, there was also a lot of background work that had to be done just to be able to memorize something." She studied *tafsīr* and Arabic grammar, and used dictionaries and grammar resource books. Memorizing did not come easily for Nada, and she utilized every tool that came her way.

After reciting it out loud twice, going over literal meaning, grammar, and *tafsīr*, she would then begin to go over the section verse by verse. "After I got that part down, I would actually go through it *āya* by *āya*. I'd usually use a recording and listen to it on repeat. I'd repeat after the *qāri'* (reciter) until I could do it on my own. Add another *āya* and do that until I could get *that* whole *āya* down, and then I'd just start combining. Every time I'd have a chunk, I would stop and go through it again several times. I didn't have a set number, it was just really until I felt super comfortable with it.

"After I memorized, for example, a new page, I would have to take a break and come back to it—see if I still remembered it. If I didn't, I would have to go through the process again and re-memorize it until it really stuck. I tried writing it, and that didn't work for me personally. I tried just memorizing off of sound, not visual, which actually made me realize that I am more of an audio learner, so that is something that helps me."

Nada would memorize three pages at a time at first, and later moved up to about five pages. She struggled to hold more than that in her mind during her first run-through of the Quran. She saw that first memorization as the first step in a life-long process. And so she continues to learn and work on holding more and more each time she reviews the Quran.

Her methodology for reviewing also relies on her aural learning skills. "I always put the Quran on repeat. Just a page. As I'm driving, I just say it with the recording. Then I focus on about five pages a week. I memorize those really, really, really well before moving on. That's what's been going well for me lately."

The process of keeping up with her own review and re-memorizing while teaching and living her busy life is a challenge for Nada. She is continuously looking for teachers to recite to, has utilized online programs, and teachers from a variety of ethnic backgrounds, "On my own, I've noticed I get stuck a lot. I'm not going to move on until I know it really, really, really, really well, so I end up not moving on and just staying on one sura for a very long time. A lot of times things like that happen." So she seeks a mentor, teacher, or anyone who will help to keep her on track.

Pointers

1. Understand your learning style.
2. Listen and recite.
3. Recite on your own.
4. Learn the meanings.
5. Learn the grammar.

6. Memorize verse by verse, learning each one and then repeating them together until they become a solid section.

Advice

Nada's advice to anyone with the memorizing itch is to go for it. "I would say everyone has their own struggles in their life. Everyone has obligations, whether you're a girl or a guy. If you have the time and dedication to do it, then go for it. There's nothing to stop you—of course with Allah's *tawfīq*."

She highly recommends that students of the Quran find out what their learning style is. She gives her students suggestions, but her biggest tip is, "Do what works for you." She is an aural learner, but knew many people who needed to write down the verses if they were going to truly memorize them. She even knew kinesthetic learners who had to recite their verses while walking or doing housework. Everyone is different, and each learner needs to experiment with what works best.

One of her teaching methods is the "Twenty numbers game." She puts twenty different numbers in a bowl, and the student picks a number and then repeats what they are memorizing that many times before moving on to the next part. This makes repetition fun, but it still does not work for everyone. "Just be in touch with what works and be aware of how things are going. Keep track."

In the end, however, Nada implores other women and girls to not give in to fear. "Don't let fear keep you from going after it. I think that's a common thing. Either the fear of having to teach, or the fear that comes with seeing it as a burden, or the fear of being called by certain labels, or whatever it is. There's just always this fear surrounding memorizing the Quran. Don't let that get in the way of what's really important." The fear of being called a *ḥāfiẓa* was a common theme among many of the women I interviewed, and Nada had this to say about it: "Perhaps women shy away from being called a *ḥāfiẓa* for fear of developing the spiritual illness of *riyā'* (braggartism), but just as there is concern for people's opinions in showing off, there is also the idea of *not* doing something because of what people will say." And all fear should be conquered when it comes to memorization.

Tips For Review

1. Listen, listen, listen, listen.
2. Find a teacher to recite to, work with a mentor.

8. Maheen

Maheen memorized the Quran between the ages of ten and fourteen. At the time of our interview, she was seventeen years old, with fond memories of the memorization process.

Like many other children, she memorized the short suras as part of her early learning. But at ten years old, her parents registered her for a *ḥifẓ* program that was integrated into her school day. They gave her the choice to continue or leave at any time, but Maheen said, "I decided to stay because it was just a really fun and amazing journey. I wanted to finish it."

Maheen was in a unique program based on motivational activities and kindness. "Our teachers made a big effort to make us happy. They never wanted us to be upset, and they would always tell us how much we should love the Quran, how much we should appreciate it."

The teachers' goal was for the children to love the Quran and the process of memorizing. They would discuss explanations of the verses in ways that children could understand. They would include stories of the Prophet ﷺ and general excitement about the blessings in life. All of this they would tie back to the Quran and the process of memorizing.

"My teachers were really sweet. Every time we finished our memorization or finished reviewing, they would give us candy to show that they were proud of us, and to show us what we'd accomplished; they'd kind of give us a reward. Every time someone finished five *ajzāʾ*, they would have a huge party for them. They would get food, and we would end class early and just have fun! We'd play games!"

But it wasn't all play and laughter; there were times when Maheen wanted to give up. When she felt frustrated, or when she fell behind, she would consider quitting, "I'd just feel really upset, and I'd just want to quit. But then I realized that I wanted to do it, and that I should finish doing it."

Maheen has seen tangible results in her young life. Growing into her faith with the Quran helped her become serious about practicing Islam. She was never distant from her religion, but memorizing the Quran gave her focus for her prayers and offered her a foundation from which to make life choices. "During and after memorizing the Quran, I was more focused on my prayers and what I shouldn't do as a Muslim, and what I should do."

Maheen has some concerns about how people react when they find out she is a *ḥāfiẓa*. "I don't mind that people know, but sometimes I feel shy saying it because some people go a little crazy. Like, 'Oh, *mashallah, mashallah*!' I don't really like it when people are like that with me." Along with excited responses, Maheen was concerned that some people expected a *ḥāfiẓa* to be unlike 'normal' people. "Sometimes people expect a lot after you've memorized. Like they expect you to be a better person, they expect you to do extraordinary things, but that's not always the case."

Maheen remembered her journey fondly. Even though her program was designed to bring forth a feeling of happiness through the activities and fun-loving spirit of the faculty and staff, her most pronounced memories were related to her own accomplishments. "One thing that really stuck out to me was being able to recite a *juzu*ʾ without having any mistakes. We had tests every time we finished a *juzu*ʾ, and I felt really proud if I got zero mistakes on a *juzu*ʾ."

Maheen is still young, and she plans to include more Quran learning in her future. *Tafsīr*, Arabic, and other classes that will help her understand what she has learned are on her horizon. She has a competitive spirit, and her brother has recently moved far forward in the Arabic language, so Maheen hopes to catch up and surpass him.

Maheen was blessed in that nobody ever tried to stop her from memorizing the Quran. She had support from both her immediate and extended family. She was also in a community in which memorization of Quran is valued. And lastly, it helped that she was in a program with other girls her age.

Method

Because Maheen was in a program, she had special time carved out each day for memorizing. The classes were designed for individual work on memorizing and recitation. At home, they would review the pages they'd learned at school.

"In the morning, I would have my normal academics like math, science, reading and social studies. Half the day was that and the next half was the memorization. We would be in the program for about four hours, and maybe two and a half hours were for memorization."

Pointers

1. Join a fun program!
2. Carve out a special time in your day for memorizing and reciting.
3. Use time not specified for memorizing to review.
4. Have fun while memorizing!

Advice

Maheen's positive attitude about her memorization experience was uplifting, but her advice to others was serious and sober. "First of all, it's not easy. It's not something a lot of people do, and there will definitely be a lot of hard things that will come, and some pressure, maybe, depending on family and friends and stuff." She advises young memorizers to review continuously. She found memorizing in the first place easier than later review, so for those just starting out, she encourages them to start their review right away.

Maheen had very specific advice for the memorizer: "Start off slowly. You don't have to do full pages every day. It really helped me when I would listen to *shuyūkh*, like on an iPad or an mp3. If you listen to it a few times, it's easier to memorize."

Maheen also encouraged new memorizers to pay attention to their friends. It is a new and intense path, and not everyone will understand. Friends will ask you out and you either will not be able to go, or won't want to. She says, "Make sure to keep good company, too, because my friends, some of them weren't great company, and that was kind of affecting my *ḥifẓ* because sometimes they would say, 'Oh, why do you have to go? Come hang out with us.' And I would want to go with them, so that affected me a lot. Lastly, again, always keep up with your review." She added, "I would say it's better if you start a little bit younger. Because when I started, I was in middle school, so it was harder to balance everything. Maybe start around eight."

Tips

1. Review constantly.
2. Choose your friends carefully.
3. Start before ten years old.

9. Umber

Umber was born and raised in Pakistan. Her story begins shortly after she completed high school. She found herself in a transitional phase when her planned course of study did not pan out, so, since she would not be able to start anything else until the next September, she decided to join a sewing program for the summer. The class was on the bottom floor of a large building that housed all kinds of home economics classes for girls, including crochet, sewing, and a beauty parlor.

"The top floor was for Quran memorization. My mom took me for the sewing [class], and I probably stayed there for a week or so. I was exploring the building that first week, and I went to the top floor. [After that] I started skipping the sewing part and observing the Quran class instead!

"The Quran teacher was very nice. She let me hang out and observe, and if I had any questions, she would answer me nicely. She never made me feel uncomfortable for sitting there or asked me what I was doing there. When I finally approached, she said, 'Why don't you just start, if you're not doing anything. Let's see if you can do this.'

"The beginning was good, and the Quran was just amazing, and my family didn't know until I was about ten *ajzāʾ* in. But after that, it got really hard, towards the middle. It gets really, really tough, and you don't feel like you're going anywhere. And my *ustādha* got married and left, so it was hard at that time. It took a while, a few months, for me to get back to where I had been."

Since Umber did not tell her family about what she was doing initially, she had to be discreet about her memorizing, "My dad is an early bird kind of person. He would wake up for Fajr and go for a walk right after praying and come back. My mom is not exactly an early bird. She likes to sleep in. She'd wake up with my dad and pray Fajr and just go right back to sleep till 8:30 or 9:00. But my dad was awake, and he would see me because we lived in a small apartment—there wasn't a place I could just sit securely and memorize. And you know, in order to memorize, you have to say it out loud and it has to be a quiet environment so you can focus.

"So I would just close the kitchen door and no one could hear me. But, one day, my dad came back from his walk after Fajr and he wanted some water or something, so he just walked in the kitchen and saw me sitting on the floor memorizing. And he was like 'What are you doing?'

"So I say, 'I'm just reading Quran.' It happened a couple of times, and then he asked me what was going on, and I said 'I don't know. I'm doing this.'

"They were supportive, but my mom wanted me to go back to university and finish my studies. I just needed some time before I wanted to go back. My dad was supportive, though. He was very supportive of what I was doing."

It wasn't that Umber's mom wasn't supportive, but, "She didn't get the whole concept. To be honest, she never believed in me, that I could finish something. And I had kind of proven that to her by not getting into med school. So she thought I would just leave this in the middle, too, and then I'd have wasted a year." Umber's mother wanted her to go back to university, pick a major, and finish a degree or something.

For Umber, in spite of her mother's concerns, the Quran was taking care of her, "The time of life I was in, I was quite lost. I had no idea. I just felt connected [to the Quran]."

The Quran focused Umber. She began to grow a sense of curiosity about *tafsīr* and Arabic. As she memorized more and more, learning the depth of its meanings became more and more important. She also found her peace. "I feel like at the time I started it, I was very lost. When you had your heart set on one thing and it falls through, it's hard. And I didn't have a backup plan. And then the parents are expecting so much from you, and then all of a sudden, the light just switches. It just lifted me up. I was very down, but it lifted me up, and I realized that there were many other things that I could do in my life."

Method

As for the specific method Umber used to memorize, she explains: "In the [program] I went to, we were usually given about a page to memorize. I would usually go for two to three hours. And I'd always memorize ahead if I could. The method would be repeating an *āya* over and over until you know that you know it. To pass a *juzu'*, you could only make two mistakes.

"We would also do what we called a *dawr* (circle) among the students where they will listen to each other recite and review. Like if I had only memorized one *juzu'*, I would repeat it every single day. If I couldn't do the whole *juzu'*, maybe I'd do a half of it or a quarter part of it, but I would repeat it every day besides the regular *sabaq* (memorization).

Umber reviews at the mosque. Now that she is married and has children, she struggles to find time at home, so she chose a place where she can concentrate. Her review is focused on straightforward recitation, but she hopes to learn Arabic soon, in order to begin to understand more of what she has memorized.

Pointers

1. Work on one page at a time.
2. Join a program for support.
3. Work with peers, sharing progress.

Advice

"This is a mission of love, and it's the most noble thing to do." Umber encourages everyone to walk on the path of memorizing, to ignore the naysayers and those who would pile on the guilt. She herself struggles to review at this stage of her life, but she knows life is about stages and she will have more time later. It is a blessing and a gift to have memorized it at all.

She does, however, strongly recommend that students of the Quran focus some time on learning the Arabic language. She is encouraging her own children to learn Arabic first, and memorize second.

For some people, memorizing is a trophy, and Umber discourages this kind of thinking. "You memorize it one time and that's it. You earn that trophy. You put it on your shelf and you're done... It takes persistence to be with the Quran all the time."

Umber also advised parents to be role models for their children. She sees many of her friends encouraging their children toward Quran, but she wishes they would begin with themselves. "I think parents should be involved in learning with their kids. Learning the Arabic if they can, learning the suras here and there. Even though they are older, it doesn't mean they should stop. They should be working with the children to motivate them and help them get the importance of it. Aunts and uncles, too. Whoever is involved in their lives should be role models." So everyone should memorize! It can be a family affair.

Tips

1. Ignore negative people.
2. Learn Arabic.
3. Think of memorizing as a lifelong endeavor.
4. Don't ask your children to memorize without memorizing yourself.

10. Suha

Although Suha grew up in Syria, it was not until she had been living in the US for nineteen years that she decided to memorize the Quran. "Growing up, I was introduced to *aḥkām* (rules of *tajwīd*) through the public school system in the seventh grade. You just learn the rules, but you don't really apply them. I had a musical ear and I could imitate the reciters. I think that helped me in applying the rules."

When she started memorizing, Suha was thirty-six years old and married with two kids (ages five and two and-a-half). She was also working part-time. She was busy, but she was not fulfilled. "I wanted to do something, but what got my attention was a local Quran program. They advertised it like 'If you do one page, in two years you'll be done. If you do two pages…' When I looked at it in numbers and pages and saw what you could accomplish if you're consistent… I think that was the trigger that got me to see if I could do it or not."

She was also hoping for blessing and peace in her life. The Quran offered Suha intellectual challenge, a personal challenge, and a spiritual boost. She was not too busy to memorize, she was too busy not to.

Method

Suha woke up two hours before the rest of her family and used that time to memorize. The rest of the day she spent reviewing what she had memorized in the morning. She learned both self-discipline and patience.

"I never quit, even if I went on vacation with my family. It was something I committed to daily, nonstop."

Suha recited to a sheikh who gave her recitation time daily. Sometimes he would stop her new recitation and insist on review. Other times he would ask her to recite large amounts of previously memorized material. When she was doing new pages, she reached four pages a day.

"You feel the blessing of waking up for the Quran. It's something I miss. I remember when my kids were really little, they would fall asleep while I [was] reciting, and one time my son said, 'When is the sheikh gonna call?' He used to wait for the nightly recitation I would do [for] the sheikh."

Pointers

1. Wake up early, before the rest of your family.
2. Use the early hours for memorizing.
3. Spend the rest of the day in review.
4. Recite at night.
5. Repeat.

Advice

Suha advises memorizers to approach the journey of memorization in a relaxed manner. She emphasized that it was a spiritual journey, full of enlightenment. Stress should not be a part of the journey. Unlike university, where exams and graduation lead to employment and a career, memorizing the Quran leads to love, peace, and contentment. She hoped that women embarking on their journey would find a relief from stress, not more stress, along the way.

Tips

1. Approach the Quran with love.
2. Don't get caught up in competition or stress.
3. Be consistent.

11. Nasreen

Nasreen was born and raised in Pakistan but moved to Ireland when she was twenty-nine years old. She is a doctor by trade, but after she had multiple children, she took time off to stay at home with them. At the age of forty, she had four children ranging in age from eleven to fifteen, and it was a busy time for her, as her children were busy with programs that required them to be dropped off and picked up. She was also taking Islamic studies classes herself. It was at that point that she decided to start memorizing the Quran.

She had already learned *tajwīd* before, and was part of a *ḥalaqa* that met once a week to study *tafsīr*. One of the senior students suggested that they memorize Surat al-Baqara. They started as a group of twenty, but that number quickly dwindled. Nasreen and her friend, the only two who did not give up, completed Surat al-Baqara and then decided to move on and memorize Surat Āl ʿImrān. They met almost every evening at 8:00 and recited their page to each other. After Surat Āl ʿImrān, they decided to continue and eventually were able to do two pages a day. After two and a half years, they'd both completed their first memorization of the Quran, *al-ḥamdu lillāh*.

Nasreen's story highlights the importance of good *ṣuḥba* (companionship). While many people from the *ḥalaqa* did not continue, two dedicated people formed a bond that got them through.

Nasreen faced resistance and people's objections. "People did say it's not good because you'll do it and then you forget, you know? But I think it is good to be connected and, you know, Allah ﷻ knows how much we can do."

Becoming a walking Quran was an "amazing feeling." And it gave her the gift of Quran. "Last night, I was on a one-hour drive back home and there was a big storm. At that time, I couldn't read even from my phone because nothing was working, but I started reading what I could from Surat Luqmān, and it was such a good feeling that you don't need the Quran with you. And especially in your salat it makes a big difference. You can recite different suras and it helps your concentration in salat."

Method

Nasreen memorized in the early mornings. Before bed, she would read through the portion she planned to memorize the next morning, and then she used the time before and after Fajr to memorize. She then recited what she had learned in the morning throughout the day in her prayers and recited to her friend in the evening.

Listening was also an important part of her method. "I used to listen to the same lesson all day. You know. Keep playing that while I'm cooking. While I'm driving. That really helped."

Pointers

1. Use the early mornings for prime memorizing time.
2. Spend the day listening to what you are working on memorizing.
3. Recite whatever you are working on in your prayers.

Advice

Nasreen felt that intention was the most important thing in beginning the journey of memorizing the Quran. The hadith 'recite and ascend' kept her motivated. "I imagine I am climbing up there and I keep on reciting and reciting and keep going up."

She finds that most of the women she talks to are more concerned about their children and don't even think of themselves as being able to memorize. She advises them to just make the intention and start, even if it is only one *āya* a day. "You find that then you get motivated. Two verses. Three verses. Five verses."

Tips

1. Put yourself first when it comes to memorizing.
2. Make sure you memorize something every day.
3. Visualize yourself moving up the scales, and let that motivate you to work harder.

12. Anne

Our next story is of an American convert who loves the Quran deeply and speaks of it with so much passion, gratitude, and love that I could feel it over the phone. She is someone who makes you want to go pick up your *muṣḥaf* right that moment, read, memorize, and explore the Quran. What I especially love about her story is that she did not set out with a definite intention that she was going to try to memorize the whole Quran. As you'll see, it was a journey that naturally fell into place based on her love of the Quran. But before she got to that point, she had a few other steps to take. She discovered Islam, accepted it, and had to learn a whole new religion.

Her story with the Quran starts even before she entered Islam. She lived in an area with very few Muslims and had never actually met one. "I cannot remember exactly, but I think the way I found this word 'Islam', and knew that Islam was a thing, was probably because

I read the autobiography of Malcolm X when I was about twelve. I was interested in civil rights."

Anne was an intelligent child and spent a lot of time at her local library. She began to research this new word, 'Islam.' "I went to the library and checked out the only books they had about Islam. There were two of them. This is pre-internet days, so I went through all the encyclopedias, looking up different words that had to do with Islam. This is how I was processing things and learning things and understanding things. I looked up the words Islam, mosque, Quran—any words related to Islam. I looked them up in the dictionaries, in the encyclopedias, because that was all I had.

"When I had exhausted all that, I knew the next step was to get a Quran somehow, a translation. They didn't have one in our library, and I felt I had to get one without my parents knowing."

Another young girl in school invited Anne to the mall, and she bought her first Quran at the bookstore on that day. She brought it home, sat on the back porch, and began to read. When she reached the fifth verse of Surat al-Baqara, {This is the book about which there is no doubt, guidance for those who are conscious of God} she said to herself, "Yes, man! This is it. This is it! This is true." And she became a Muslim on the spot.

Anne spent the next months reading and studying the Quran. It was like a magnet that kept pulling her back. In between classes she would read it, whenever she had to wait she would read it, and whenever she had a moment. She was not raised with any religion at all, so the simplest of religious vocabulary sent her to the dictionary. Even the word, 'worship' was a mystery to her. All during seventh and eighth grade, the Quran was her constant companion. She would read it and do her best to follow it.

"The way I understood salat was a whole different thing, because I didn't have any specific information on exactly how to pray, I just had a very vague description. So I made up something based on what those descriptions in the book said to do. They said something like, 'You have to recite a part of the Quran.' So I would. (In English, of course!) There were different portions of it that I had underlined that I would say as I was praying. That was part of the beginning for me."

The next step for Anne was to try to learn Arabic. She went to

Georgetown, intending to study linguistics, and began her first semester of Arabic.

"After my first semester of Arabic at Georgetown, I started understanding a lot of the Quran. That was so exciting for me. I felt like it was my language. It doesn't feel like a foreign language to me. Even now, if I'm listening to something I don't understand in Arabic, it still feels like it is my language, it belongs to me somehow, and I already know it, even if I don't understand it." Learning Arabic opened Anne's heart to the Quran even more. "It was when I first really started understanding it that I was possessed with this desire to contain it, to carry it." She was now on a path to memorizing—though she did not know it yet.

Life happened. She got married, gave birth to four children, and lost touch with the part of herself that had been so deeply connected to the Quran. "For ten years, I didn't memorize Quran. My husband would stay awake after Fajr and read Quran, and I would almost feel angry. Like, 'You're able to just sit and work on Quran, but I've been up all night with the kids. I am all the time with the kids.' There were a lot of times when my kids were really little when I had been awake all night with them and was dead in bed after Fajr."

When Anne entered her thirties, she looked around and realized that she had been neglecting herself for ten years. She feared that her daughters would grow up thinking that Quran was something that only men do, and she resolved to restart her journey with the Quran. She began to work on her recitation and started memorizing Surat al-Kahf.

"That is also the time I first started seriously reading in Ramadan. I had tried before, but it would take me forty-five minutes to an hour to finish one *juzu'*. Then, once I started memorizing more and getting used to reading the Quran more often, I was like, 'I really need to make a point to read the Quran in Ramadan and finish it in Ramadan.'"

She decided that she would finish the entire Quran that Ramadan, and though it was a Ramadan when they moved house and faced numerous obstacles and struggles, she did it.

Her accomplishment bolstered her to continue. She attended the first Rabata *tajwīd* retreat, worked hard, and determined to continue her studies. Memorizing the entire Quran became a palpable goal.

Once Anne solidified her decision to memorize the whole Quran, she tried to make the hour drive to her teacher's house each week for recitation, but it became difficult due to weather conditions and family responsibilities. That didn't stop her, though. She had spent a long time waiting for the 'perfect' circumstances to avail themselves, and she finally realized that they were never going to knock on her door. Money worries, children's colds, bad weather, and flat tires would all continue to happen, but she needed to keep working and pursuing her goal to memorize the Quran.

She spoke of her memorization moments as time with God. She enjoyed filling her world with the sounds and reverberations of the Arabic letters and words. She spoke about the meaning in letters we see in calligraphy and her heart's connection to meanings she felt in the sounds of the Quran.

Anne has a beautiful way of answering the question of how one should manage fear of 'forgetting' the Quran: "My goal is that I don't die until I have at least memorized every part of the Quran once, because I want to feel like the whole Quran is going to be my friend in the grave. Even if I 'forget' parts of it, Allah can bring that out from me. It is in there somewhere, right? It is not going to go away completely. When people try to scare you with the idea that you are going to forget it, they don't realize that you obviously don't forget it completely."

Anne used the Quran to set up an environment of peace and love in her home. She and her daughters are introverts and don't like big crowds, so they avoid *tarāwīḥ*. Anne didn't want her daughters to miss out on the blessing of the prayer in *jamāʿa* (in a group), though, so she set up a prayer area in her home and led her daughters in prayer. She believes in the importance of hearing Quran recited from the hearts of live people that we know and love. "When I die, I want my daughters and my grandchildren and my son and these people that I raised to remember me reciting Quran."

Anne spoke about how memorizing the Quran has changed her, "It has made me feel that Islam is truly for me. Sometimes I think converts go through life feeling that Islam is something that they watch other people do, because they feel like they need special knowledge to participate fully. But I feel like the Quran is the great equalizer, because everybody can do it. It is always there, and you don't have to go someplace special to get to it.

Method

Anne spends a lot of time reciting and listening to the Quran, and this helps her memorize. She also points out that, any time she has trouble memorizing a part, she goes deeply within herself and examines her own shortcomings. If we want the Quran to be part of our hearts, we need to know what needs to be removed from our hearts before it will enter, so much of her method includes deep work on herself.

Pointers

1. Memorize every day.
2. Read daily and whenever you get a chance.
3. Don't let life get in the way.
4. Take note when a verse is difficult; there may be something you need to change within yourself before you will be able to move forward.

Advice

Anne's advice to everyone is to remember that there is no perfect time. Not before kids or after kids, not before graduating or after. She advises us all to 'just start.'

"You have to put that foot on the road and go down it. Then continue on it, even if it is a small amount per day. You may be moving a little bit, but you are still moving." When we stop procrastinating, we immediately change from a woman who might one day memorize to a woman who is memorizing now. Do it for yourself and your spiritual growth, and do it for the children, the youth, and the other women in the community who need to see you.

Anne also advises us to remember that we must interact with the

Quran every day.

"One time I heard a sheikh say that if a day goes by and you have not interacted with the Quran, then you really cannot consider that to be a successful day. That stuck with me. If I ticked off all these boxes on my to-do list, but I did not interact with the Quran, I need to hurry up and fix that. Even if I am lying in bed and am about to turn out the light and I just pick it up real quick and read the page that I am on. Just so that I do not have that gap."

However, Anne cautions, even if we miss a day or two or even a month, we are still memorizing and should self-identify in that way. As a memorizer, you know you will be back any moment now.

Finally, Anne speaks some more about time. "It is important to value and protect your memorizing time. Even if it is scattered throughout the day. Because people don't take women's time seriously." Anne advises us all to take our time seriously and not allow interruptions. When we take our memorization seriously, others will take us seriously as well.

Tips

1. Set aside time daily for your Quran.
2. If a day goes by and you haven't memorized or read Quran, do a little bit before falling asleep.
3. Take your memorization time seriously. Don't let others label it as unimportant and feel they can interrupt you.

Chapter Four
Guilt, Goals and a Guide

So full of artless jealousy is guilt,
It spills itself in fearing to be spilt.
Shakespeare

I heard a lot from the women I interviewed around the topic of guilt and the difficulty of keeping up the Quran once it is learned, I heard concerns around Arabic and meaning, and I heard concerns about review. This guilt was difficult for me to hear about. It seems that we have created a culture that foists guilt on women surrounding the accomplishment of the Quran, instead of a celebratory attitude.

In my experience, memorizing the Quran built a unique relationship with it. You get to know the *āyāt* in a very personal way. Arabic is very important but does not substitute for memorization. If you compare two people who both know Arabic, and they both worked on understanding the Quran through *tafsīr* for example, the one who memorized is a step ahead. For example, if somebody's reciting, you know what they are saying. Maybe you can finish the verse, or maybe you just feel it 'dancing in your heart.' The memorizer's relationship with the Quran is valuable and beautiful.

This relationship is priceless, and guilt should not be part of the conversation. If you are working on the Quran, whether you are reviewing or you are working on understanding it or learning the Quran in Arabic, you have not forgotten the Quran.

I think the fear is that people will memorize it and then never read it again. Or they will not care to continue. But the Quran itself lends purpose and a need to understand it. The desire for it to be part of your life grows with every verse.

Guilt and the Fear of Forgetting

A significant barrier, affecting not just women but everyone, is the misinterpretation of the hadith about punishment for forgetting memorized Quran. Many use this as an excuse not to memorize in the first place or to discourage others from memorizing. I know people who were literally stopped from memorizing and told, "Don't memorize the Quran, because, if you forget it, it's a worse sin."

Having gone through a *khitma* one time, I knew there was no way that one could remember the whole thing just by memorizing it once. It is a lifelong commitment of consistent review. There are times where you will know one part of the Quran better than the other because you are focusing on reviewing that part. Does that mean that you are counted as someone who has forgotten the Quran?

I asked all the women I interviewed this question, and they all unanimously agreed that the warning about losing the Quran means leaving the goal altogether.

Forgetting

In *al-Dalīl ilā Taʿlīm Kitābi Allāh al-Jalīl* (The Guide for Learning the Book of God the Exalted), Hassana bnt. Muhammad Nasir Ad-Din Al-Albani and Sukaina bnt. Muhammad Nasir Ad-Din Al-Albani examine different aspects of what 'forget' means in relation to the Quran. They start out describing 'forgetting' as an issue that every teacher will encounter with his/her students regarding what they are currently learning or what they have learned in the past. They explain that learning any subject exposes it to being forgotten over the passing days, months, and years. Therefore, they describe forgetting as the enemy of learning and state that it is worse when it concerns the words of Allah that the student has learned.

They then differentiate between two types of forgetting. There is the forgetfulness which is rare and transitory, for even someone who perfects their learning can come across forgetful moments at times. We see examples of this in the sunna. Aisha ﵂ said that the Prophet ﷺ heard a man reciting and said, "God grant him mercy! He has reminded me of a verse that I was led to forget."[29] It is not befitting to say, "I forgot such-and-such verse" based on the hadith narrated by Abdallah b. Mas'ūd ⬥, who stated that the Messenger of God ﷺ said, "Let none of you say, 'I forgot such-and-such verse.' Rather, it is something he was led to forget."[30]

Of course, the Prophet ﷺ did not mean that he had forgotten the verse, but that the man had reminded him of it. The Prophet ﷺ is the vessel of revelation, and Angel Gabriel reviewed it with him yearly to ensure its accuracy. In other words, his joy at being reminded of the verse and his words "he has reminded me of a verse that I was led to forget" refer to the verse and reminder at that time, not a deeper forgetfulness, for the Prophet ﷺ did not forget or leave out any verse of the Quran. Nonetheless, it is a great comfort to us, as our own forgetfulness is a source of frustration that is tempered by the Prophet's joy at remembering.

The Blessing in Forgetting

The second kind of forgetting is that which is excessive and can lead to errors in what has been learned. Al-Bani and al-Bani highlight forgetting as a phenomenon that everyone who memorizes the Quran is exposed to, but they quote Dr. Fahd al-Rumi, who believes that there is wisdom behind the phenomenon. While it is a trial and tribulation for the heart of the worshipper, it is also an important exercise in growth. The difference is substantial between a heart that is attached to the Quran and is routine in its recitation versus a heart that was attached to the Quran at the time of memorization but then, just like boiling water cools down, its motivation wanes, it is distracted, and then it forgets. A believer carries a heart that is deeply attached to the Quran and is willing to do the work necessary to hold on to it.

Preserving one's memorization requires a great deal of recitation, and this recitation leads to more reward for every letter that is recited. If we never forgot what we memorized, we would not feel the need to recite a great deal, and we would lose out on much reward, so the fear of forgetting is a blessing. And indeed it is! Not wanting to forget has pulled me back time and again to reviewing my Quran, reciting it at night, and finding people willing to hear me recite again and again.

Preventing Forgetfulness

1. Sincerity and asking for reward from Allah ﷻ alone.
2. *Istighfār*—or seeking forgiveness.
3. *Du'ā'* and begging from Allah ﷻ to have the Quran firmly planted in the heart of the *ḥāfiẓ*.
4. Repeat, repeat, repeat.

The Duty of the Teacher

1. Making clear what the causes of forgetting are for the *ḥāfiẓ*.
2. Helping the student to avoid those things.
3. Working on one's *nafs* to rid oneself of those things.
4. Teaching the student how to protect herself if the above happens.

The Goal to Remember

Every memorizer hopes to remember the Quran forever. What is the actual *sharī'a* ruling regarding people who memorize the Quran and then forget all or part of it?

There is no *ṣaḥīḥ dalīl* from the *sharī'a* on the punishment for forgetting Quran, but it is not of good manners for the *ḥāfiẓa* to become heedless of recitation of the Quran or to leave her covenant with it. She has to take it upon herself to maintain a daily *wird* (amount) that she reads as part of a routine. This will help prevent forgetting and deepen her understandings of the Quran, which will motivate her to live by its meanings.

One of the most important analogies regarding memorizing the Quran is found in the hadith narrated from al-Bukhārī by Ibn 'Umar ﷺ, that the Messenger of Allah ﷺ said: "The likeness of the one who memorizes the Quran is that of the owner of a hobbled camel. If he tends to it regularly, he will keep it, but if he lets it go, he will lose it."[31] Just as one must feed, water, and tend to the health of a hobbled animal, one must likewise nurture the Quran they have memorized. It takes review, practice, and recitation to keep and build on what one memorized the first time around. One may struggle with this when circumstances get hard or life responsibilities increase. The one who forgets due to an illness, for example, is forgiven of course, and the one who memorizes a portion of the Quran and then forgets it because of work or distraction is not in sin. Imam Nawawī deemed it to be not *ḥarām* (prohibited), but *makrūh tanzīhī* (disliked, but not deserving of blame)[32]. What is blameworthy is to stop caring about Quran and carrying the mission in your heart.

Not only is there the benefit of the reward for recitation in general, but each individual letter garners its reciter reward, as Muhammad b. Ka'b al-Quraẓī narrated: "I heard Abdullah b. Mas'ūd saying: 'The Messenger of Allah ﷺ said: "[Whoever recites a letter] from Allah's Book, then he receives the reward from it, and the reward of ten the like of it. I do not say that *Alif Lām Mīm* is a letter, but *Alif* is a letter, *Lām* is a letter, and *Mīm* is a letter."'"[33]

حدثنا محمد بن بشار حدثنا أبو بكر الحنفي حدثنا الضحاك بن عثمان عن أيوب بن موسى قال سمعت محمد بن كعب القرظي قال سمعت عبد الله بن مسعود يقول قال رسول الله صلى الله عليه وسلم: (مَنْ قَرَأَ حَرْفًا مِنْ كِتَابِ اللَّهِ فَلَهُ بِهِ حَسَنَةٌ، وَالحَسَنَةُ بِعَشْرِ أَمْثَالِهَا، لَا أَقُولُ الم حَرْفٌ، وَلَكِنْ أَلِفٌ حَرْفٌ وَلَامٌ حَرْفٌ وَمِيمٌ حَرْفٌ)

There are unseen effects on the heart, as well, such as an increase in *khushū'* and improved understanding and insight for the one who reflects.

Some ill-informed Muslims have used *āya* 126 of Surat Ṭā-hā to scare people about forgetting Quran, {[God] will reply: 'Thus it is: there came unto thee Our messages, but thou wert oblivious to them, and thus shalt thou be today consigned to oblivion!'}[34]

قَالَ كَذَلِكَ أَتَتْكَ آيَاتُنَا فَنَسِيتَهَا وَكَذَلِكَ الْيَوْمَ تُنسَى

Al-Walīd explains this, however, as referring to someone who has left acting upon the commandments of the Quran, not someone who has memorized it and forgotten some of what they memorized. Much of this confusion comes from misinterpretation of the word '*nasiya*,' which people cite as 'to forget;' however, the *mufassirūn* have explained that '*nasiya*' in this case means '*taraka*' (to leave), because it is not of the attributes of Allah ﷻ that He forgets. It means that they have left acting upon the *āyāt*, not just forgotten them.[35]

Many of the early Muslim scholars taught that forgetting Quran can be the result of sin. Someone who memorizes the Quran is at a higher *maqām* (station or rank) compared to someone who has not memorized (in the respect of having memorized more), but if she does not fulfill the duties and manners of that rank, she will slowly slip down without her noticing; the forgetting is the result of her indifference. In this case, what the person is held accountable for is *the action that led them to become indifferent to the Quran*. So to protect one's connection with the Quran, a person has to be vigilant about all of her affairs. For a slip in a seemingly unrelated aspect of one's life—which could include anything from one's character to one's prayers to guarding one's senses—can lead to a diminution in her relationship with the Quran.

The reverse is also true. The desire to hold on to one's love for the Quran and connection to it can motivate the one who has memorized to be vigilant in all aspects of her life, so as not to be trialed with a break in that valuable connection and the loss of the gift. Sheikh Abū Dharr al-Qalamūnī said that memorizing the Quran is the beginning of knowledge, and every *āya* that is memorized is an open door to Allah ﷻ, and every *āya* that is memorized and forgotten is a closed door between you and your Lord. After reflecting on all the above, it strikes me that there is mercy in that there are not detailed guidelines about how much a *ḥāfiẓa* must review every day. The important thing that is stressed is to maintain a connection with the Quran, always. The other thing that struck me was the realization that many people hold on to a harsh view of Allah ﷻ when it comes to memorization instead of focusing on His mercy. Of course, some fear is good to keep us vigilant about not leaving our review of Quran and our forever connection with it, but it should not be paralyzing or cause us to leave the journey.

The authors' beautiful summary concludes with reminding us that many people get caught in the whispers of Satan, who tells them not to memorize the Quran because, if they forget it, they will have sinned. They urge us to remember the *āya*, "Fight, then, against those friends of Satan: verily, Satan's guile is weak indeed!"[36] So memorize Quran, for in it there is *khair*. Have high hopes for remembering and keep in mind that Allah ﷻ is as His servant thinks of Him.[37]

My First Guide to the Quran

I cannot talk about advice for memorizing Quran without including my very first teacher for *ḥifẓ*. She has always been an inspiration to me as her love for the Quran shines through, even so many years after she initially memorized. She is devoted to reviewing daily, no matter how busy she is with her volunteer work and extensive community involvement.

Ustādha Azza has been in the Quran 'business' for many years. She has taught professionals, students, and stay-at-home moms. She believes that each person should create her own schedule. She does not put much stock in speed, but rather in persistent consistency. She strongly recommends getting up early before everyone else and using that time to review what one had memorized the day before. She also suggested keeping a daily record of accomplishments. "Definitely, you must document what you are doing and your progress."

After all these years, she still has her own journal and continues to keep a record of her review. But for new memorizers, she recommends a ratio of 80/20. For every hour of memorizing, 80% should be for new material and 20% for old.

Ustādha Azza reminded me that neither women nor men should be memorizing for the sake of leading a prayer. The false argument that men memorize to lead *tarāwīḥ* is a fallacy. "She might not be leading *tarāwīḥ* for men, but she definitely can lead it at home with her family or lead *tarāwīḥ* for other women. Also, she can lead other prayers for women; it doesn't have to be *tarāwīḥ* only. That's one. Second, this is not why we are memorizing Quran, even the men. If this is their intention for memorizing to lead *tarāwīḥ*, to be the leaders in the prayer, then what if they don't lead the prayer? Then what's the point? This should not be the intention, and I don't think there's a separation between, or differences between, males and females in this regard."

She mused that there are many different motives for people to memorize the Quran, "And [in] this the Prophet ﷺ never discriminated between male or female; we both do *qiyām*, we both read Quran. She is not going to be busier than him. They are both busy. But definitely she is in need... I mean one of them, mom or dad, male or female, she might be the one who needs it more, because she's going be teaching it to the younger generation and having the patience to do it."

So here we are at the crux of the matter. As our communities have discouraged women from memorizing, we have fewer mothers who have a relationship with the Quran, which has a return effect on society. Who is teaching our next generation? Ustādha Azza points out that women usually have more of a tendency to share their learning, and so are more dependable as teachers of the next generation. Hence the importance of women *ḥāfiẓāt* for all of society.

Advice

Ustādha Azza shared some parting advice straight from her heart. "Number one, just trust Allah. When you do something for His sake, He will open all the doors of blessing and success for you. And remember the hadith narrated by ʿAṭiyya from Abū Saʿīd, that the Messenger of Allah ﷺ said: 'The Lord, Blessed and Most High is He, has said: "Whoever is too busy with the Quran for remembering Me and asking Me, then I shall give him more than what I give to those who ask."'"[38]

عن أبي سعيد الخدري أن رسول الله صلى الله عليه وسلم قال: (مَنْ شَغَلَهُ الْقُرْآنُ عَنْ ذِكْرِي وَمَسْأَلَتِي أَعْطَيْتُهُ أَفْضَلَ مَا أُعْطِي السَّائِلِينَ)

Ustādha Azza said that she asks Allah to give her whatever He deems she needs. She is busy memorizing, reading and reviewing the Quran and usually doesn't have time to ask for personal things, so she relies on His generosity and wisdom in knowing what is good for her.

"So what I'm saying is, do what makes Allah happy and put your trust in Allah that He will make you happy. The best medicine is Quran; it treats everything. And this is not something I invented... Allah says in the Quran itself,

قُلْ هُوَ لِلَّذِينَ آمَنُوا هُدًى وَشِفَاءٌ

"Say; it is, for the believers, a guidance and a cure."[39]

"So it's really a cure. I'm not talking only physical—you read Quran if a person is going through something. I'm talking psychological and spiritual. So yeah, my advice is that, regardless, even if the person does not have the commitment to memorize, at least to have a friendship, a relationship, with the Quran, minimum let's say, ten minutes, fifteen minutes a day. Do not put the Quran on the side and leave it as a decoration."

She remembered a friend of hers who started memorizing and then stopped, thinking she was too old to finish before she died. Ten years later, she started again and realized that working on it was more important than finishing it. "And those ten years, if she [had] invested them, she would have been done now."

Ustādha Azza was especially confident about the ability of women to memorize the Quran. She said, "I believe that women are more passionate and more persistent, and they have a stronger will. I'm sorry, I don't mean to discriminate against men, but this is what I believe, that women are, as I said, (sic) when she sets a goal and she believes in it, she can do it. And, as I said it's, *wallāhi* (by God), a blessing in her home, for herself, for her family, everything."

Pointers

1. Make *du'ā'* to ask Allah to help you with it.
2. Be consistent. You must be consistent.
3. Make a strong intention.
4. Do not move to a new part without setting a schedule to

review. Reviewing what you memorize is as important as memorizing.

5. Make a schedule based on your lifestyle.
6. Use the early morning hours.

Chapter Five
The Stories That Weren't

It is never too late to be what you might have been.
George Eliot

The women I spoke to who had completed the memorization of the Quran were often surprised to hear about other women who had been discouraged from the path of memorization. While some had successfully fended off the naysayers, many had never heard a negative word. But what of the dozens of women who were so discouraged that their journey was put to an end?

I heard two such stories, of women who had a gift for being able to memorize, but their journeys were cut short because of the words of others.

Halima

In the Indo-Pak culture, it is customary that every child learns how to read Quran at a young age and recite the whole thing by somewhere between the ages of six and ten. When they start, they are thrown a 'Bismillah' party, and when they complete their reading of the entire Quran, they have an 'Ameen' party. It is considered a rite of passage in a way, and the children are celebrated with cakes, presents, and dinner. It is common for the young reciter, after the Ameen party, to go forward without opening the Quran very often—and this can last far into adulthood.

Halima's story was different. After she had her Ameen party at the age of twelve, her father, noticing that she was very good at reciting Quran, was interested in having her pursue memorization. He consulted with a friend of his who was a *ḥāfiẓ*. This man told him that memorizing Quran is not something that girls do. So her father dropped it for a while and told her daughter that she had no need to pursue memorizing.

She told me that since she was so young at the time, she didn't ask too much about it. But this changed as she got older. "I was like, 'Wait.'"

Halima never let her connection with the Quran fall to the wayside. Her mother and grandmother always encouraged her to recite Quran, although the idea of memorization never occurred to them. She started working on her *tajwīd* with different teachers and eventually ended up in my living room, first as a student of *tajwīd*, and then a student of memorization.

It had been many years since her dream of becoming a *ḥāfiẓa* had been shelved. Now she would start again—older, wiser, and newly determined.

Sanam

Sanam has a similar story, although it ended differently. "I think I was around fifteen years old. I was going to the mosque. I'd been going for a few months, and I was one of the older girls who was there. Usually girls stop going to the mosque around the time they start their period, which was eleven for me, so I had dropped out of my local mosque. Then I was traveling over to another mosque in the city because that was one where they had female teachers. It was more appropriate for older girls to go to that one. I was going there with my little sister as well, who was with the younger kids. The older girls were around my age and a little bit older maybe. Up to about seventeen. They were girls who—I don't know if you have this same kind of thing, but in my city in particular we have mosques that are run by family dynasties. There's one main family in charge of running that mosque, and everyone is involved in that.

"These older girls were part of the family that was running the mosque. The imam's daughters were the ones who were memorizing

Quran. I was trying to make the most of my time there, and I was trying to learn the best I could. I was thinking about it, I thought it over, had a conversation with my mom at home, and I said, "I think I want to start memorizing the Quran like the older girls there, and my intention is to do as much as I can." My mom was really pleased with that, and so she was like, "Okay, I'll go speak to your teacher at the mosque."

"I remember my mom came into the mosque with me that day and asked to speak to this teacher. We went into a separate room, a big, empty, large room with no furniture in there. You know the type with the green carpet and a few bookshelves with Quran and things like that on it. I was really excited. I was looking forward to this really huge decision that I had made for myself. I know that my mom was really supportive as well. She was speaking to this teacher and she said, 'Okay, my daughter wants to start memorizing Quran and would like for you to help her do that. What would that entail?' All these kinds of questions. The woman responded, and she just kind of looked more concerned than anything else. I think she was giving advice in a most sincere and thoughtful way, where she just said plainly to my mom that, 'Is this really what you want your daughter to do? Because it's a good intention for girls to want to memorize Quran, but you also have to think about when she's older. When she gets married, if her husband beats her, then it's like he's beating the Quran.'"

Sanam's mother spoke evenly and quietly, and still insisted that she wanted to support her daughter in memorizing. But the light had been put out, and, though Sanam began to memorize, she petered out and quit because of the attitude and lack of support she found.

The shocking nature of the suggestion that somehow it would be bad to beat a woman *because she memorized the Quran* and not because *she is a sacred human being* was lost on the people in the mosque and much of Sanam's community.

It was much later in life that the real ugliness behind her story dawned upon Sanam. "I suddenly realized, 'Oh my gosh, that is really messed up. That is extremely twisted beyond all common sense and reason.'"

Halima and Sanam's stories are tragedies of community. Sanam's story was so difficult to hear that I struggled to incorporate it into this book! But how many other stories like this are there? How many other girls were discouraged from memorizing the Quran when they clearly had an inclination and ability to do so?

Are you a story that never was? Or has not happened yet? Is it because of belittlement from others or because of your own lack of motivation and commitment?

Be a story that was. Start today.

Chapter Six
Roadmap

A goal without a plan is just a wish.
Antoine De-Saint Exupery

While every woman's story is unique; each path woven together can help us see our way to memorizing. The following are the most important commonalities amongst the successful memorizers that I interviewed. I've included personal tips and some general advice from other writers about memorizing Quran.

Intention

It goes without saying that any time we embark on any project or undertaking for the sake of our *deen*, intention is key. Not only at the beginning, but also throughout and at the end. It needs to be renewed consistently. When one starts such a lofty undertaking, Satan will be fast on her heels to try and stop her. When he attacks one's intention, it usually takes one of two forms: it might be through trying to corrupt her intention, or, even more underhanded, it might be by making her believe her intention is not correct, and therefore she should stop until she fixes it. So remember, even if you are concerned about your intention, never stop doing a good deed. Keep an eye on your intention, do your best to keep it pure, but do not stop the deed. Just keep renewing the intention.

Sheikh Muhammad al-Habash cites three considerations important in memorizing Quran in his book 'How to Memorize the Quran.' The first one is sincerity. He reminds us all that the Quran is God's word, and trying to memorize it for fame, or to win a contest, or any other worldly reason, is void of benefit. He goes on to say that if the one striving to memorize the Quran feels that s/he is oriented towards

Allah ﷻ, s/he will find her or his ability to memorize stronger and will find more success.

Tajwīd

It is important to work on fixing one's recitation prior to memorizing large portions of the Quran, not least because it is difficult to fix mistakes that have been memorized. Spend some time with a qualified *tajwīd* teacher before moving on to memorization. Oftentimes people want to jump to memorization, yet they have not perfected their *tajwīd*, and they end up memorizing things incorrectly, which costs them time and frustration in the end.

I recommend completing a whole *khitma* in *tajwīd* with a qualified teacher before moving on to memorization. It takes more time—it may add on months or even years to your preparation before you start memorizing—but it is well worth it in the end. *Tajwīd* protects one from making errors in the book of Allah ﷻ. If one cannot properly differentiate between the letters *kāf* and *qāf*, and uses them interchangeably or is unable to pronounce one of them, it could change the meaning of some words. For example, if one pronounces *qalb* as *kalb, her recitation would come out meaning dog instead of heart. So* instead of reciting beautifully about people's hearts, one would be melodiously chanting about people's dogs.

You might ask yourself, why does it sound like this? Why is this *tajwīd* rule being used here? Maybe it's something I need to pay close attention to. You may notice that the *āyāt* that speak of the mercy of Allah ﷻ utilize rules that lead to a very peaceful rhythm, whereas the *tajwīd* rules in the *āya* about the damning of Abū Lahab create a chopped, harsh, almost angry sound.

Teacher

Find a teacher who lives as close to you as possible. The best way to stay on track is to be accountable to someone, and the best way to be accountable to someone is to have a teacher with whom you have set up weekly appointment times. The closer they live to you, the easier it is to ensure that you keep your appointments. Nowadays, digital platforms are an option as well, if one cannot find a teacher in her locality. However, it should be a last resort, as it is always better to meet face to face with one's teacher.

Consistency

Many people want to memorize the Quran, but don't see it as a possibility because they don't have the time or the opportunity to go away somewhere and focus on just that. Although it is nice to be able to devote a chunk of one's life to this goal, it is not a requirement for memorizing success. There is no 'perfect time' to do it. Life happens and will continue to happen. Allah ﷻ loves those deeds that are consistent, even if they are small. So pick a certain amount of time that you wish to devote each day to your goal, and try to stick with it no matter what. It could be twenty minutes. As some of the sisters mentioned, it is a good habit to make this the time after Fajr, as this is the time that is mentioned in the Quran.

وَقُرْآنَ الْفَجْرِ ۖ إِنَّ قُرْآنَ الْفَجْرِ كَانَ مَشْهُودًا

{*The Recitation at Fajr, Verily, the recitation at dawn is indeed witnessed.*}[40] The nice thing about this time, other than it being the time specified in the Quran, is that it is usually a time of little distraction. School and work have not yet started, and children are usually still sleeping. Some people like to do it at the other end of the day, before bed. This works for them because it becomes a ritual before retiring for the night. It is another time in the day when one might find distraction-free moments. This is not to say that those twenty minutes cannot be at any other time of the day. Of course they can! Figure out what works best for you and try to stick with it.

Ṭahāra (purity of self—physical and metaphysical)

The words of Allah ﷻ can only be held in a pure heart. Guard your senses so that your heart is not filled with the dirt and grime of the *dunyā*, but is preserved for His beautiful words. Don't allow your eyes to invite in images that will float through your head when you are trying to keep a visual of the page you are memorizing in front of you. Don't let poisonous words compete with the flowing language of the Quran. The more you protect yourself, the more the words of the Quran will stay within you.

Eat Right

Make sure to eat a well-balanced diet with vegetables, fruits, and adequate protein, and avoid foods that will leave you feeling tired and cloud your mind. Using all that brainpower burns up calories, so make sure you get enough of them, and that they are healthy ones.

Patience

Patience, patience, patience—I was told when I first started memorizing that it is difficult in the beginning but that it gets much easier as you go. I was told that Surat al-Nisāʾ is the hardest, and once you are through memorizing that, you are scot-free. But the truth is that everybody's experience is different. I did not find Surat al-Nisāʾ to be much harder than some of the other suras, and furthermore, I found that suras with longer *āyāt* were actually easier for me than suras with shorter but more numerous *āyāt* (like in the last third of the Quran). So it was more of a consistent, steady pace for me throughout. I did have the advantage of better Arabic by the end, but it still took time and effort. I did see people who had *futūḥ* that allowed them to memorize thirty or more pages a day, however, if that doesn't happen for you, it's okay. Consistency is more important than the amount.

Use It

Recite what you have memorized in your *qiyām*. In the Shāfiʿī school of thought, you can put your *muṣḥaf* on a stand and read from it if you need to. If you can recite what you memorized in prayer, it is a good way to gauge whether you know it or not.

'Tie Up Knowledge with Writing'

One of the most helpful pieces of advice I received was to write down every page of the Quran without looking at it, after I had memorized it and before moving on to the next page. This helped immensely by becoming my gauge as to when I had practiced the page enough to know it well.

Listen and Listen

Listening to Quran helps. Even if it is playing in the background, it can help to hear it over and over. One can pick up a surprising amount just by listening.

Pace Yourself

It is a good idea to practice what you've memorized at the same speed that you will be reciting. Sometimes when practicing, we tend to recite quickly, so that we can review more in the time we have allotted for it. Then, when it comes time to recite to your teacher, slowly and with perfected *tajwīd*, it can be difficult to remember anything. This often happens with suras you recite daily, as you tend to read them very fast and it becomes so automatic, you can no longer slow down.

Choose One *Muṣḥaf* Style

One of the first pieces of advice my teacher gave me was to make sure that I used an Uthmani script *muṣḥaf* and to use one that starts and ends each page at an *āya* break. This helps to create a picture of the page in your mind, and using the same *muṣḥaf* throughout also helps, as your brain takes a mental picture of the page.

Learn Arabic

The Arabic language is the language of the Quran, and you will be making your job much easier when you learn at least perfunctory grammar and vocabulary. It is not a prerequisite to memorizing the Quran, but Arabic is a blessing for the one memorizing. Many people memorize the Quran without understanding a word of it. This is part of the miracle of the Quran, and one of the ways Allah fulfills His promise to preserve it:

إِنَّا نَحْنُ نَزَّلْنَا الذِّكْرَ وَإِنَّا لَهُ لَحَافِظُونَ

{Indeed, it is We who sent down the Quran and indeed, We will be its guardian.}[41]

Allah ﷻ has made the Quran easy to memorize. Think about how hard it would be to memorize a few pages of English text word for word. Even if it is your first language, you might still find it difficult. However, learning Arabic will help you along the way and bless you with a deeper understanding of God's words.

The Quran is Your Teacher

I've heard this often. My teacher spoke about how certain forms of worship are sensitive barometers for your state. The Quran is one of them, and especially the memorization of it. Everything you do (or don't do) during the day affects your ability to not just memorize, but even to sit down with the Quran and try! This includes the protection of the senses (protecting one's eyes from seeing spiritually destructive images, one's ears from hearing unacceptable speech, one's tongue from speaking inappropriately, and one's hands from doing wrong). The senses are all a window into the heart, and any one of them can affect the state of the heart—and hence the ability to memorize the Quran. One of my teachers explained that the *āya*:

لَّا يَمَسُّهُ إِلَّا الْمُطَهَّرُونَ

{None touch it except the purified.}[42]

means that if you have sinned without repentance, you will find that you just cannot sit down to read Quran. First of all, you may not even think about doing so, and secondly, if you do, you may find yourself getting distracted on your way and going off to do other things.

Make a Schedule

One piece of advice that was stressed by my teachers was to be mindful about one's schedule and to actually create a chart to keep track of all the different aspects of one's time and actions. The chart could consist of spots for the five daily prayers, for an amount of time spent with Quran (or a checkmark to indicate that one spent any amount of time with it). I have always struggled with this because I am not a chart kind of person. But when I do stick with it, it is helpful for many reasons. It makes me feel more accountable and helps keep me on track. See a sample chart in the appendix.

Tawba

One of the first things I was told as I decided to embark on this path was that the first step is *tawba*. Sin is heavy. It is difficult to move forward when one is weighed down by a heavy past. For some, moving forward may involve starting to pray the five daily prayers, for some it may mean a change in dress, and for some it may mean improving one's character. Everyone is different. Everyone has that thing in her life that needs attention, that needs to be changed. All of us need to work on our weaknesses, whether we want to learn Arabic, study *fiqh*, embark on a journey with the Quran, or just live our best lives. And the first step in improving and lightening our load is *tawba*.

Duʿāʾ

Duʿāʾ is the brain of all of our worship. It is no different for memorizing the Quran. While it is important to work hard, *duʿāʾ* humbles us and reminds us that in the end, it is Allah ﷻ who opens doors for us and allows us to do *khair*. My teachers used to say of *tahajjud* that if you wake up and pray at night, consider it as an invitation from Allah ﷻ to stand before Him.

Internal Motivation

Sheikh al-Habash mentions this as the second of three foundational principles of memorizing. He states that, although the promise of rewards and prizes is acceptable, if that is the only driving force, then when the gifts, or the desire for those gifts, is gone, the motivation will be gone also. This is especially important for children, as they may not be able to conceptualize the delayed rewards in Heaven, so in the beginning they may need external motivation in the form of gifts. Also, it should be a positive experience for them. It is something that the adults in their lives should make a big deal of. We celebrate so many different occasions. The best presents should be for the Quran, so that children see how important it is. In this way, they will internalize that motivation as they grow, *in shāʾ Allāh*.

Minimal Distractions

When I spent my year memorizing in Syria, I was lucky that smartphones were not that common. It was easy for me to focus and disengage from distractions. It is much harder now, with smartphones and social media. Not only does one have to be careful about the time that can be wasted on the distraction of social media, but with many social media platforms, one runs the risk of being exposed to things she shouldn't see. For that matter, one also has to watch what she 'says' on social media. Your smart phone has direct access to your senses. It can grab your heart in the blink of an eye. Learn to be disciplined about its use during your memorization time and in general.

Better Late Than Never

I look back at how fresh my mind was and all the free time I had as a child and young adult, and I cringe at the time wasted. But then I stop myself because it came to me when it was supposed to. Everything in life happens on Allah's ﷻ time. 'Better late than never' is so true when it comes to the path. Regret can be paralyzing, so leave it behind. It has no place in the suitcase that you're packing for the future. Be around people who have already memorized Quran and people who are currently memorizing—Seeing people who have reached the end goal makes it seem doable, and the presence of other memorizers helps keep everyone motivated. A little healthy competition is also beneficial at times.

Change of Lifestyle

Realize that you may need to change your lifestyle during times of intense memorizing. You may miss out on 'fun' at times. Although it's important to maintain a balanced life, there will be times when your memorizing will require more time than others. It may mean a few years. That time is not lost. It's time spent building a foundation.

Don't Forget the Heart Work

Whether we are memorizing Quran or not, we should always be striving to work on our hearts, striving to be better human beings. This means fighting negative thoughts and feelings and working hard to prevent the diseases of the heart, like arrogance, vanity, bad opinions of others, etc., from taking hold.

The Quran is Not An All-or-Nothing Endeavor

Of course we all want the satisfaction and reward that comes with memorizing the entire Quran. But if that goal seems unattainable, like scaling Mt. Everest, it doesn't mean we should give up before we even start. Any time that you spend with the Quran, whether it is learning the Arabic alphabet, learning *tajwīd*, reading, or learning *tafsīr*, will garner you both rewards from Allah and benefits in your life.

Jump in Where You Are

Remember that memorizing Quran is a path, and that most of the time that path does not begin with memorizing right off the bat. It starts out with learning the Arabic alphabet. It includes learning *tajwīd*. Different people will insert themselves onto the path at different points. Just make sure you insert yourself in there somewhere.

I did not set out initially to memorize the Quran; I set out to learn Arabic. From there, my path swerved towards working on *tajwīd* and then getting my *ijāza* in *tajwīd*. The decision to memorize grew naturally, organically, through the love that I developed by spending so much time with the Quran.

There is No Perfect Time

Although it would be nice to have dedicated time that one can spend focusing on Quran only, that is not always possible. Make it a part of your life no matter what stage you happen to be in.

Do Not Be Afraid

Don't let fear get in the way of memorizing the Quran. There's so much fear surrounding it. The fear of being labeled, the fear of thinking of it as a burden. The fear of not being able to do it at all. Satan uses fear to prevent people from doing good things. Don't let him fool you like that.

Never Give Up

And don't let people discourage you. Focus on your goal and ask Allah ﷻ to help you with it.

Be Grateful

Always be grateful for any moment you spend with the Quran and any amount you memorize. Consider it an invitation from Allah ﷻ to spend time with His words.

Keep a List of Hadiths About the Blessings of Reciting and Memorizing Quran

I included a few in the above stories, and here list some more:

1. Sālim narrated from his father ؓ, who said that the Messenger of Allah ﷺ said: "There is to be no envy except for two: A man to whom Allah ﷻ grants wealth, and he spends from it during the hours of the night and the hours of the day, and a man to whom Allah ﷻ grants (memorization of) the Quran, so he stands with it (in prayer) during the hours of the night and the hours of the day.'"[43]

حدثَنَا أَبُو اليَمَانِ، أَخْبَرَنَا شُعَيْبٌ، عَنِ الزُّهْرِيِّ، قَالَ: حَدَّثَنِي سَالِمُ بْنُ عَبْدِ اللَّهِ، أَنَّ عَبْدَ اللَّهِ بْنَ عُمَرَ رَضِيَ اللَّهُ عَنْهُمَا، قَالَ: سَمِعْتُ رَسُولَ اللَّهِ صَلَّى اللهُ عَلَيْهِ وَسَلَّمَ يَقُولُ: «لاَ حَسَدَ إِلَّا عَلَى اثْنَتَيْنِ: رَجُلٌ آتَاهُ اللَّهُ الكِتَابَ، وَقَامَ بِهِ آنَاءَ اللَّيْلِ، وَرَجُلٌ أَعْطَاهُ اللَّهُ مَالًا، فَهُوَ يَتَصَدَّقُ بِهِ آنَاءَ اللَّيْلِ وَالنَّهَارِ»

2. 'Uthmān ؓ narrated: "The Prophet ﷺ said, 'The best among you [Muslims] are those who learn the Quran and teach it.'"[44]

حَدَّثَنَا شُعْبَةُ، قَالَ: أَخْبَرَنِي عَلْقَمَةُ بْنُ مَرْثَدٍ، سَمِعْتُ سَعْدَ بْنَ عُبَيْدَةَ، عَنْ أَبِي عَبْدِ الرَّحْمَنِ السُّلَمِيِّ، عَنْ عُثْمَانَ رَضِيَ اللَّهُ عَنْهُ، عَنِ النَّبِيِّ صَلَّى اللهُ عَلَيْهِ وَسَلَّمَ قَالَ: (خَيْرُكُمْ مَنْ تَعَلَّمَ القُرْآنَ وَعَلَّمَهُ)

3. Anas ؓ tells us that the Prophet ﷺ said, "The believer who reads the Quran and abides by it is like a citron—its smell is pleasant and its taste is pleasant. And the believer who does not read the Quran and abides by it is like a date—it has no smell and its taste is sweet. And the hypocrite who reads the Quran is like basil—its smell is pleasant and its taste is bitter. And the hypocrite who does not read the Quran is like a colocynth—its taste is bitter and it has no smell.[45]

عَنْ أَنَسٍ، عَنْ أَبِي مُوسَى الأَشْعَرِيِّ، قَالَ: قَالَ رَسُولُ اللَّهِ صَلَّى اللهُ عَلَيْهِ وَسَلَّمَ: «مَثَلُ المُؤْمِنِ الَّذِي يَقْرَأُ القُرْآنَ كَمَثَلِ الأُتْرُجَّةِ، رِيحُهَا طَيِّبٌ وَطَعْمُهَا طَيِّبٌ، وَمَثَلُ المُؤْمِنِ الَّذِي لاَ يَقْرَأُ القُرْآنَ كَمَثَلِ التَّمْرَةِ، لاَ رِيحَ لَهَا وَطَعْمُهَا حُلْوٌ، وَمَثَلُ المُنَافِقِ الَّذِي يَقْرَأُ القُرْآنَ مَثَلُ الرَّيْحَانَةِ، رِيحُهَا طَيِّبٌ وَطَعْمُهَا مُرٌّ، وَمَثَلُ المُنَافِقِ الَّذِي لاَ يَقْرَأُ القُرْآنَ كَمَثَلِ الحَنْظَلَةِ، لَيْسَ لَهَا رِيحٌ وَطَعْمُهَا مُرٌّ»

4. Abu Huraira ﷺ narrates that the Prophet ﷺ said, "A group of Muslims does not come together in one of Allah's houses, reading Allah's book and studying it amongst themselves, but that serenity descends upon them, and mercy envelops them, and the angels encircle them, and Allah ﷻ mentions them to those who are with Him,"[46] meaning the angels and prophets.

عَنْ أَبِي هُرَيْرَةَ قَالَ قَالَ رَسُولُ اللَّهِ صَلَّى اللَّهم عَلَيْهِ وَسَلَّمَ : « مَا اجْتَمَعَ قَوْمٌ فِي بَيْتٍ مِنْ بُيُوتِ اللَّهِ يَتْلُونَ كِتَابَ اللَّهِ وَيَتَدَارَسُونَه بَيْنَهُمْ إِلَّا نَزَلَتْ عَلَيْهِمُ السَّكِينَةُ وَغَشِيَتْهُمُ الرَّحْمَةُ وَحَفَّتْهُمُ الْمَلَائِكَةُ وَذَكَرَهُمُ اللَّهُ فِيمَنْ عِنْدَهُ »

5. The Prophet ﷺ said, "Verily Allah ﷻ has kindred amongst people." The companions asked, "Who are Allah's people?" He said, "Those who carry the Quran are Allah's family and His elite."[47]

عَنْ أَنَسِ بْنِ مَالِكٍ رضي الله عنه قَالَ: قَالَ رَسُولُ اللَّهِ صَلَّى اللَّهُ عَلَيْهِ وَسَلَّمَ: (إِنَّ لِلَّهِ أَهْلِينَ مِنَ النَّاسِ قَالُوا: يَا رَسُولَ اللَّهِ، مَنْ هُمْ؟ قَالَ : هُمْ أَهْلُ الْقُرْآنِ ، أَهْلُ اللَّهِ وَخَاصَّتُه)

Pitfalls to Avoid

1. Memorizing the Quran is a forever endeavor. Be careful about thinking that when you complete your first *khitma*, you are done. It's something you will have to make time for, for the rest of your life.
2. When you get derailed, don't panic. It does happen. Life happens. Whether it is school, work, or family obligations, inevitably things come along that require a change of schedule. Sometimes it is hard to keep up with the twenty minutes per day because other things fill up the time that would have been used for that (sometimes it is sleep that takes up the time). Once one lets go of the daily twenty minutes, it is sometimes disheartening and difficult to get back on track. There may be feelings of guilt and inadequacy. But it is important to be able to put those feelings aside and just get right back into the habit again. Even if that means starting out with one *āya* a day, or allotting five minutes a day instead of the twenty, thirty, or a whole hour.
3. Terminology is also important when talking about memorizing Quran. It is dangerous to say things like, "I've finished memorizing the Quran." One never 'finishes' memorizing. One could say, "I've finished my first time through," or "I completed my first *khitma* in memorizing," but it will be a lifelong journey. Although it is exciting to complete things, and we celebrate when someone completes their first *khitma* with parties and crowns, trophies and other gifts to encourage people to continue, it is important not to forget the importance of the journey itself. One of my close friends, who started memorizing the Quran at a very young age and devoted all her free time to Quran for years, eventually got her *ijāza 'al-ghaib*. She often told me not to worry about rushing things, as the "ending" was anti-climactic, and she sometimes wishes she could go back to the journey. She told me to enjoy it and savor it, because it is the time with the Quran and the strengthening of one's relationship with Allah ﷻ that really matters. It is not a race.
4. Never give up—anything in life that is worthy can be difficult. There will be *āyāt* and pages that you struggle with. Don't get

discouraged on down days. Remember that every day is a new day, and you can pick yourself up.

5. Spiritual highs—when one does a great deal of any form of worship, oftentimes there is a feeling of peace and/or other gifts from Allah ﷻ. With the memorization of Quran, this can be quite intense. Our teachers always reminded us, however, not to fall into the trap of worshipping those feelings. They emphasized that we always worship Allah ﷻ. It is a fine line, and walking it requires a constant renewal of intention.

6. Don't give in to the thought that you are not 'good enough' to become a *ḥāfiẓa*, therefore, you may as well not try. This is akin to one saying she is not good enough to wear hijab or good enough to do xyz. This train of thought is a trick of Satan to prevent you from doing something good. We are not perfect and will never be. In fact, our beloved Prophet ﷺ said, "I swear by the One in Whose hand is my soul, if you were a people who did not commit sin, Allah would take you away and replace you with a people who would sin and then seek Allah's forgiveness so He could forgive them."[48]

عَنْ أَبِي هُرَيْرَةَ قَالَ قَالَ رَسُولُ اللَّهِ صَلَّى اللَّهُ عَلَيْهِ وَسَلَّمَ: (وَالَّذِي نَفْسِي بِيَدِهِ لَوْ لَمْ تُذْنِبُوا لَذَهَبَ اللَّهُ بِكُمْ وَلَجَاءَ بِقَوْمٍ يُذْنِبُونَ فَيَسْتَغْفِرُونَ اللَّهَ فَيَغْفِرُ لَهُمْ)

7. With this in mind, one could look at it the other way. The more imperfect we are, the more we are in need of all the reward we can get. And even *reading* Quran gains us ten for each letter, so *in shā' Allāh* memorizing helps us even more.

8. Beware of the "OK" plateau. This is a point that people reach in learning when your brain decides, "You're OK with how good you are at something, turn on autopilot and stop improving."[49] In the 1960s, two psychologists, Paul Fitts and Michael Posner, described three stages that people go through when acquiring a new skill. The first stage, the 'cognitive stage,' is when you intellectualize the task and discover new strategies to accomplish it more proficiently. The second, 'associate stage,'

is when you start concentrating less, making less major errors, and become more efficient. The third stage is the 'autonomous stage,' when you basically start running on autopilot because you figure you've gotten as good as you need to get at the task.[50]

9. After completing a first *khitma*, the challenge of which brings with it a certain energy and motivation, people may feel lost or struggle to stay motivated to continue reviewing. One way to avoid falling into this trap is to try and stay in the 'cognitive phase' instead of falling into the 'autonomous phase.' Anders Ericsson, an expert performance psychologist, determined that experts are separated from the rest of the crowd in that they engage in 'deliberate practice.' They try to stay out of the autonomous stage while they practice by doing three things: "Focusing on their technique, staying goal-oriented, and getting constant and immediate feedback on their performance."[51]
10. This can be seen in the difference between amateur musicians and pros in that the former spend more time playing music, whereas the latter focus on specific, difficult parts of pieces.
11. This can translate to Quranic memorization, especially after completing one's first *khitma*, in that you can set new goals, preferably ones that are more challenging. If you used to connect two pages maximum every time you recited to your teacher, you could try to increase that to five. You can even set larger goals, such as wanting to memorize through the entire Quran a certain number of times. Or you could focus on particular *āyāt* or suras that you struggled with and focus on improving those. Continuously challenging yourself can keep you moving forward.

Chapter Seven
The Etiquette of Proper Recitation of Quran[52]

Verily, the one who recites the Quran beautifully, smoothly, and precisely, will be in the company of the noble and obedient angels. And the one who recites with difficulty, stammering or stumbling through its verses, will have twice that reward."

Prophet Muhammad ﷺ[53]

Reading and memorizing the Quran is a lifetime habit that gets more beautiful by the day. In the struggle to improve the beauty of our recitation—we learn *tajwīd*, listen to reciters, increase our practice, etc. And in order to improve the beauty of the *act of* reciting we look to increase our good manners with the Quran. Children's books tell us that good manners are to improve our relationships with people, likewise good manners and proper etiquette with the Quran improves our relationship with it and with God. The best deeds are those that are both sincere and correct. A sincere deed is one done for Allah alone, and a correct deed is one done according to the rules of *sharīʿa*. Therefore, a reader should follow certain principles when reciting. The scholars have agreed on a number of etiquettes of reciting Quran:

1. Have *wuḍūʾ*! The reader should be in a state of ritual purity. Meaning she should be free of that which breaks minor ritual ablution (*wuḍūʾ*) and that which breaks major ritual ablution (*ghusl*). *Wuḍūʾ* is a spiritual state. It is a preparation that opens our heart to the recitation of God's words.
2. Recite and practice in a *ṭāhir* place: The place (in which she reads) should be *ṭāhir*—legally pure and free of *najāsa* (any impure substance). We respect the Quran by reciting it in clean and tidy places.

3. Start with *ta'awwudh* (seeking refuge in Allah from Satan) whether you are reading from the beginning of a sura or the middle. This is according to Allah's words:
4. "So when you recite the Quran, seek refuge in Allah from Satan, the expelled."[54]

فَإِذَا قَرَأْتَ الْقُرْآنَ فَاسْتَعِذْ بِاللَّهِ مِنَ الشَّيْطَانِ الرَّجِيمِ

5. Say, "In the name of God, the Gracious, the Merciful" (بسم الله الرحمن الرحيم) at the beginning of each sura, except Surat al-Tawba.
6. The reader should read with spiritual openness (*khushū'*) out of respect for the Quran. Allah says: {If We had sent down this Quran upon a mountain, you would have seen it humbled and breaking down from fear of Allah...}[55]

(لَوْ أَنزَلْنَا هَٰذَا الْقُرْآنَ عَلَىٰ جَبَلٍ لَّرَأَيْتَهُ خَاشِعًا مُّتَصَدِّعًا مِّنْ خَشْيَةِ اللَّهِ
وَتِلْكَ الْأَمْثَالُ نَضْرِبُهَا لِلنَّاسِ لَعَلَّهُمْ يَتَفَكَّرُونَ)

7. The reader should read with thoughtfulness, reflecting about the meaning of what she reads. {Then do they not reflect on the Quran...}[56]

(أَفَلَا يَتَدَبَّرُونَ الْقُرْآنَ أَمْ عَلَىٰ قُلُوبٍ أَقْفَالُهَا)

8. The reader should beautify her voice during reading—without pretense. Barā' b. 'Āzib said: "The Messenger of Allah ﷺ said: 'Beautify the Quran with your voices.'"[57]

حَدَّثَنَا شُعْبَةُ، قَالَ: سَمِعْتُ طَلْحَةَ الْيَامِيَّ، قَالَ: سَمِعْتُ عَبْدَ الرَّحْمَنِ بْنَ

عَوْسَجَةَ، قَالَ: سَمِعْتُ الْبَرَاءَ بْنَ عَازِبٍ، يُحَدِّثُ قَالَ: قَالَ رَسُولُ اللَّهِ صَلَّى اللَّهُ عَلَيْهِ وَسَلَّمَ: (زَيِّنُوا الْقُرْآنَ بِأَصْوَاتِكُمْ)

9. And from Abū Huraira: "He is not of us who doesn't recite the Quran in a melodious voice."

عن أَبِي هُرَيْرَةَ قَالَ : قَالَ رَسُولُ اللَّهِ صَلَّى اللَّهُ عَلَيْهِ وَسَلَّمَ: (لَيْسَ مِنَّا مَنْ لَمْ يَتَغَنَّ بِالْقُرْآنِ)

10. The purpose of beautifying your voice is to facilitate the understanding of the meaning, to move anyone that might hear it, and to appreciate the beauty of the style and words. Reciting it melodiously to entertain (as a song would) is *ḥarām* (forbidden). A truly beautiful and melodious recital is that which depends on correct pronunciation and perfect application of *tajwīd* rules, along with a spiritual connection and commitment to the Quran.
11. Recite the Quran in *tajwīd*.
12. Hold back the urge to yawn during reading until the urge to yawn is gone.
13. Respond to the truth of Allah's words and witness the call and testament of the Prophet ﷺ.
14. Once you have begun, do your best to avoid interruption of your recitation from moment to moment with human discourse, unless absolutely necessary (like returning the greeting of *salām*—the Islamic greeting).
15. The reader should ask Allah for His bounty at a verse of mercy and seek refuge with Allah at verses of warning.
16. Brush your teeth before reciting.
17. Sit up straight, and don't lean back.
18. Dress for reciting the Quran as though intending to visit a statesman, for the reciter is engaged in an intimate conversation.

19. Face the direction of prayer (*qibla*).
20. Rinse the mouth with water if coughing and mucus or phlegm is coughed up.
21. Recite leisurely and without haste, pronouncing each letter with distinction.
22. Use your mind and attempt to understand what is being said to you.
23. Pause at verses that refer to God's bounty in order to long for God and ask for His blessing, and at verses of His punishment to seek God's saving grace.
24. Pause at the narratives of bygone people and benefit from their example
25. Remember that each letter is rewarded as ten good deeds, so pronounce each letter with clarity.
26. When finished, to attest to the truth of God and His message, "*Ṣadaqa Allāhu al-Aẓīm,*" (God, the Almighty, is true).
27. Do not leave the Quran open if it is set down after reciting. This act of respect has been developed by Muslim cultures with the idea that we want to protect the *muṣḥaf* from dust or any damage that might come to it if carelessly left open.
28. Do not place other books on top of the Quran; rather place it higher than all books.
29. Do not place the Quran on the floor when reading or otherwise.
30. Do not compete in volume when reciting it.
31. Do not toss it when handing it to another.
32. Begin anew when a complete recitation has been finished (even if just with a few verses).

Conclusion

The best of you are those who learn the Quran and teach it.
Prophet Muhammad ﷺ[58]

Throughout this book, we have heard stories of faith, hope, and commitment. We have also heard stories of struggle, disappointment, and hard work. We heard from women who grew up memorizing Quran and women who started their journeys much later. We heard from women who were born into Islam and women who converted. I hope you were able to identify with at least one of these stories, and that it has inspired you to begin a relationship with the Quran or rekindle a relationship that may have fallen by the wayside. Most of all, I hope that you find strength in that relationship, and an anchor to hold your faith down on the days when it falters.

Even though there were ups and downs in most of the stories, and the path was not always easy, there is one word I hope will always spring into your heart when it comes to the Quran, and that word is 'joy.' The end result of our worship, and especially memorizing Quran, is that our hearts should emanate joy, our words should be filled with love for others, and our actions should reflect the character of the Prophet ﷺ, of whom Aisha ﵂ said, "His character was the Quran."[59]

Appendix One
Sample Worship and daily habit schedule for memorizing Quran

	Monday	Tuesday	Wednesday	Thursday	Friday	Saturday	Sunday
5 Daily Prayers							
Tahajjud							
Memori-zation 20 minutes							
Dhikr							
Surat al-Kahf on Fridays							
Surat al-Baqara							
Surat al-An'ām							
Backbiting							
- - - -							
- - - -							
- - - -							

Appendix Two
Glossary

ākhira	The next life, the after life
al-ḥamdu lillāh	All praise and thanks be to God
Anse	Title for a female scholar/teacher
āya	Verse of the Holy Quran
b.	Abbreviation for *ibn*, meaning 'son of'
bnt.	Abbreviation for *bint*, meaning 'daughter of'
ḍād	The Arabic letter/sound that is not found in any other language.
deen	Religion/ way of life/ holistic approach to faith and life
du'ā'	Supplication, prayer
dunyā	The world as we see it and know it, the seen world, the world we live in
Fajr	The time of the morning prayer
fiqh	Specific rulings and directives about prayer and daily life
ḥāfiẓ (pl. *ḥuffāẓ)*	A man who has memorized the Quran
ḥāfiẓa (pl. *ḥāfiẓāt)*	A woman who has memorized the Quran
hajj	The pilgrimage to Mecca
ḥalaqa	A group of people gathered to learn
ḥifẓ	Memorization
hijab	Used in this case to mean head covering/ scarf/*khimār*

ijāza	A license to teach, traditional degree in Islamic education
ijāza 'al-ghaib	A degree in the correct pronunciation of the Quran and the memorization of Quran
imam	leader, especially of prayer or a masjid; also used as an honorary title for scholars of hadith
in shā' Allāh	God willing
jilbāb	A long over garment worn by some Muslim women
juzu' (pl. *ajzā'*)	A twenty-page part of the Holy Quran. The Quran is made up of thirty of these parts.
Juzu' 'Amma	The thirtieth twenty-page part of the Holy Quran.
keema	A traditional meat dish from the Indian subcontinent. The word may be borrowed from the Turkish *kiyma*, which means minced meat. It is typically minced beef or mutton curry with peas or potatoes.
khair	Goodness
khitma	A complete recitation of the Holy Quran
khitma 'al-ghaib	Reciting the whole Quran by heart
khushū'	Spiritual openness and focus during worship
mabrūk	A colloquial phrase shortened from '*mubārak*,' which means 'congratulations, or 'blessings'
mashallah	A phrase meaning 'what Allah has willed', used to praise and protect the one being praised
mufassirūn	Those who explain the Quran
muṣḥaf (pl. *maṣāḥif*)	The word used to refer to the Quran when it is printed in book form
nafs	Human essence; also the self-centered ego

qiyām	Supererogatory night prayers
sabr	To recite a large portion of Quran at once—to collect memorized pages together, review them, and recite them in one go
ṣaḥīḥ dalīl	An authentic proof, or reliable evidence
sharīʿa	Islamic canon law
sheikh (pl. *shuyūkh*)	A teacher or scholar: a word that refers to an elder
sīra	The study of the life of Prophet Muhammad ﷺ
subḥān Allāh	All glory be to God
sunna	The body of Islamic custom and practice based on Prophet Muhammad's words and deeds
sura	A chapter of the Holy Quran
tafsīr	The study of the meanings
tahajjud	Supererogatory night prayers
tajwīd	The science of the pronunciation of the Quran
tajwīd ijāza	A degree in the correct pronunciation of the Quran
tarāwīḥ	Supererogatory night prayers performed nightly throughout the month of Ramadan, often prayed in groups
tawba	Repentance
tawfīq	Divine serendipity
umma	Muslim community at large
ustādha	Title for a female scholar/teacher

References

Al-Bani, Hassana bint Muhammad Nasir Ad-Din, Al-Bani, Sukaina bint Muhammad Nasir Ad-Din, *Ad-Dalil Ila Talim Kitabi Allah Al-Jalil.* Beirut: Dar Ibn Hazm, 2004.

Al-Habash, Muhammad. *How to Memorize the Quran.* Damascus, Dar Al-Hikmah.

Al-Hussaini, Al-Hajjah Hayat Ali. *Useful Tips from the Science of Tajweed.* Damascus, 2000.

As-Siddiqi, Muhammad ibn Alaan. *Al-Futuhat Ar-Rabbaniyya Ala Al-Adhkar An-Nawwawiyya.* Beirut: Dar Al-Ihya.

Csikszentmihalyi, Mihaly. *Flow: The Psychology of Optimal Experience.* New York: Harper Row, 2009.

Doidge, Norman. *The brain that changes itself: stories of personal triumph from the frontiers of brain science.* Kbh.: Nota, 2014.

Edelman, Marian. "It's hard to be what you can't see" Web blog post. *The Blog.* Huffpost, 21 Aug. 2015. 2 Aug. 2017.

Foer, Joshua. (2011) *Moonwalking with Einstein: a journey through memory and the mind.* London: Allen Lane.

Harris, Dr. Russ. *The Confidence gap: A Guide to Overcoming Fear and Self-Doubt.* Boston: Trumpeter, 2011.

Mattson, Ingrid. *The story of the Qur'an: its history and place in Muslim life.* Chichester, West Sussex, UK: Wiley-Blackwell, 2013.

Nawawī, Musa Furber, and Nuh Ha Mim. Keller. *Etiquette with the Quran: al-tibyān fī ādāb ḥamalat al-Qur'ān.* Place of publication not identified: Islamosaic, 2003.

Saujani, R. (2016, Febrary 17). *Reshma Saujani: Teach girls bravery, not perfection* [Video file]. Retrieved from https://www.ted.com/talks/reshma_saujani_teach_girls_bravery_not_perfection

Endnotes

1 Abū Dāwūd, Aḥmad
2 Imam Aḥmad
3 Quran: 91:10
4 Mattson, Ingrid, pg. 141
5 Csikszentmihalyi 2009, pg. 4
6 Csikszentmihalyi 2009, pg. 3
7 ibid
8 ibid
9 *Jāmi' al-Tirmidhī*, English reference: Vol. 5, Book 42, Hadith 2914; Arabic reference: Book 45, Hadith 316
10 *Ṣaḥīḥ* – (al Bani)
11 Quran: 50:16
12 Doidge 2014, pg 47
13 Doidge 2014, pg. 47
14 Doidge 2014, pg 46
15 Doidge 2014, pg 47
16 Foer 2011, pg 38-39
17 Quran: 26:88-89
18 Quran: 19:12
19 Harris 2011
20 Quran: 11:114
21 Saujani 2016 -Ted Talk
22 Edelman 2015
23 Musnad Imam Aḥmad 12491
24 *Sunan al-Tirmidhī* 2914: *ṣaḥīḥ* (authentic) according to al-Tirmidhī
25 Quran: 22:77
26 Quran: 2:153

27 Quran: 39:10

28 Quran: 49:12

29 Bukhārī Vol 6 #5038

30 Bukhārī Vol 6 #5039

31 Bukhārī, 5031

32 Al-Bani 2004

33 Tirmidhī

34 Quran: Ṭā-Hā:20

35 Al-Bani 2004

36 4:76

37 The Prophet ﷺ said, "Allah the Most High said, 'I am as My servant thinks (expects) I am. I am with him when he mentions Me. If he mentions Me to himself, I mention him to Myself; and if he mentions Me in an assembly, I mention him in an assembly greater than it. If he draws near to Me a hand's length, I draw near to him an arm's length. And if he comes to Me walking, I go to him at speed.'" (Bukhārī)

38 *Jāmiʿ al-Tirmidhī* -Hadith 2926

39 Quran: 41:44

40 Quran: 17:78

41 Quran: 15:9

42 Quran: 56:79

43 *Jāmiʿ al-Tirmidhī*; Volume 4, Book 1, Hadith 1936

44 *Ṣaḥīḥ al-Bukhārī* 5027; Book 66 Hadith 49; Vol. 6, Book 61, Hadith 545

45 Al-Bukhārī and Muslim Book 9, Hadith 995

46 Ṣaḥīḥ Muslim Book 035, Hadith Number 6518

47 Imam Aḥmad, *Sunan Ibn Mājah* Vol. 1, Book of Purification and its Sunna, Hadith 215

48 *Sahīh Muslim* (2687)

49 Foer 2011

50 ibid

51 ibid

52 Al-Hussaini, (2000) (pg 19-20)

53 Bukhārī and Muslim

54 Quran: Surat al-Naḥl: 98

55 Quran: Surat al-Ḥashr: 21

56 Quran: Surat Muhammad: 24

57 Al-Nasā'ī

58 Bukhārī

59 Al-Bani; Book 14, Hadith 308

CPSIA information can be obtained
at www.ICGtesting.com
Printed in the USA
BVHW071424090421
604505BV00005B/440

9 780999 299036